CAMPAIGNS
THAT SHOOK
THE WORLD

For my father, the late Professor Alan Rogers.
And for Wendy, Hazel and Daisy;
thank you for all your love and support.

CAMPAIGNS THAT SHOOK THE WORLD

The Evolution of Public Relations

DANNY ROGERS

First published in Great Britain and the United States in 2015 by Kogan Page Limited

2nd Floor, 45 Gee Street
London EC1V 3RS
United Kingdom
www.koganpage.com

1518 Walnut Street, Suite 1100
Philadelphia PA 19102
USA

4737/23 Ansari Road
Daryaganj
New Delhi 110002
India

© Danny Rogers, 2015

The right of Danny Rogers to be identified as the author of this work has been asserted by him in accordance with the Copyright, Designs and Patents Act 1988.

ISBN   978 0 7494 7509 3
E-ISBN   978 0 7494 7510 9

British Library Cataloguing-in-Publication Data

A CIP record for this book is available from the British Library.

Library of Congress Cataloging-in-Publication Data

Rogers, Danny, author.
   Campaigns that shook the world : the evolution of public relations / Danny Rogers ; foreword by Martin Sorrell.
      pages cm
   ISBN 978-0-7494-7509-3 (paperback) – ISBN 978-0-7494-7510-9   1. Advertising campaigns–Case studies.   2. Political campaigns–Case studies.   3. Branding (Marketing)–Case studies.
4. Public relations–Case studies.   I. Title.
   HF5837.R64 2015
   659.1'13–dc23
                                                                                          2015031271

Typeset by Graphicraft Limited, Hong Kong
Print production managed by Jellyfish
Printed and bound by CPI Group (UK) Ltd, Croydon CR0 4YY

Brief contents

Thanks...

Jasmin Naim, my original commissioning editor, for believing in me and the book; Alan Edwards and his 2015 exhibition at the V&A 'Always Print the Myth', which provided great inspiration; and my employer Haymarket Media Group for affording me the space and time to embark on the work.

Contents

PART THREE   Modern marketing movements
with digital convergence and purpose   133

Foreword

by Sir Martin Sorrell, founder and CEO of WPP

As a business, advertising and marketing services has often done a poor job of advertising and marketing itself (there, I've said it).

This unfortunate paradox might help to explain why, in today's cost-driven corporate world, we are having to work harder than ever to convince clients of the value of what we do.

Campaigns that Shook the World is, therefore, a timely reminder of what can be achieved when individuals, organizations and brands harness the astonishing power of marketing communications.

These pages hold no comfort for those who still cling, limpet-like, to the misguided notion that a good product will – through its virtues alone – simply sell itself.

Would Margaret Thatcher have won such a resounding victory in 1979 without Tim Bell and the Saatchi brothers? Would David Beckham have become an enduring global brand without expert advice on publicity? Would Dove have evolved into a champion of female self-esteem (nearly doubling its sales in the process) without the inspired creativity of the Real Beauty campaign?

The answer in every case is an emphatic 'no'.

Few have articulated the case for marketing investment better than Jeremy Bullmore, the former chairman of J Walter Thompson London. If you haven't come across Jeremy's writing, his 1998 essay *Polishing the Apples* is a good place to start.

'To put a competitive case,' he writes, 'is to present your case – your company, your product, your idea, your policies, your proposition – as attractively as possible. It's why people buy cosmetics, why window-dressers should be well paid and why costermongers polish their apples.

'No competitive enterprise, in whatever field of endeavour, can leave its apples unpolished and still expect to win. There may still be a few who belong to the "good wine needs no bush" school of marketing but they won't be found amongst the winners and quite soon they won't be found at all.'

Danny's book identifies some of the best apple polishers in the business, and examines the role they played in many of the defining campaigns – personal and political, commercial, sporting and cultural – of the modern era.

It also makes the fundamental point that a campaign need not, and often should not, be a one-off event, a short-term phenomenon. These are stories of sustained, long-term success, backed by sustained, long-term investment in marketing communications. Lessons there, perhaps, for the over-cautious occupants of today's boardrooms.

Campaigns that Shook the World is testament to the effectiveness of great communications. It's more, though, than a welcome addition to the marketing canon. The people and campaigns it explores have shaped the world in which we live – our politics, media, culture and society – in entertaining, controversial and fascinating style.

David Ogilvy, one of the fathers of modern advertising, said: 'Unless your advertising contains a big idea, it will pass like a ship in the night. I doubt if more than one campaign in a hundred contains a big idea.' This book is all about that 1 per cent.

Introduction

Why do some politicians win election after election, while rivals fade into historical obscurity? Why do so few brands connect emotionally with their customers across the world? How did David Beckham transcend his sport and become a global brand himself? How does one Olympic Games inspire a generation? How do ageing rockers like the Rolling Stones keep reinventing themselves?

There are several factors that lead to long-term success politically, in the business world, in sport or entertainment. But most who achieve it, who gain legendary status, are outstanding communicators and have run great campaigns. This book attempts to identify the politicians, the brands and the people whose campaigns have triumphed. It examines precisely how they have connected so well with their audiences over many years. It provides the definitive case studies of those campaigns that have proven brave and innovative rather than safe and banal. In short, it celebrates a selection of campaigns that can claim to have shaken the world.

So what defines a great campaign? Campaign is a commonly used, often misused, term in marketing and media. You probably use it more than you think. But rarely are the campaigns that we all observe and discuss each day examined in detail. Did they actually work? What did they change? If triumphant, what were the elements that moved the dial? Who were the people crucial to their success? It was about time someone sorted the wheat from the chaff, the few true world-beaters from the run-of-the-mill. That is why I wrote this book.

Having spent nearly 25 years specializing in media and marketing – initially running campaigns but more often as a journalist reporting on them – it was frustrating that I rarely had time to look under the surface. Journalists tend to be complicit – reporting the top-line successes and mixing happily with the protagonists, but rarely getting the chance to study them in depth. It was the opportunity to write the definitive case studies on what I judged to be the gold standard campaigns and provide my own take on how they worked. I'm not so naïve as to see this list as comprehensive. There are of course other great campaigns that deserve such recognition. If there are some that I have missed then please do let me know at **www.CampaignsThatShookTheWorld.com**.

Uniquely, this book tells the story of modern communications through the eyes of great campaign orchestrators. Often there is a visionary leader – Barack Obama, Tony Blair, Seb Coe, Bono, Mick Jagger – but always there are communications experts, 'campaign stars' if you like, who are pivotal to their success. These gurus are absolutely representative of a generation of outstanding PR and marketing talent. I wanted to interview and celebrate some of these colourful characters, most of whom I have got to know well while editing the magazines *PRWeek* and *Campaign*. Some, like Alastair Campbell, Lord Bell and Matthew Freud, are much maligned, but unfairly so in my view. Some, like Simon Fuller, Paddy Harverson and Jackie Brock-Doyle, are hugely respected but rarely give interviews. And others, like Silvia Lagnado, the marketer who devised Campaign for Real Beauty, have not got the credit they deserve. Hopefully these pages change all that.

Yes, this book does set out to be useful and educational for people who work in PR, advertising or media, or who would like to. But it's also designed to be an entertaining, cultural read for anyone who shares my passion for politics, business, sport and music. It is, at heart, a brief story about inspirational people and their work – and how that impacts on our own lives.

Before we start, however, we must define the bare minimum requirements of a 'campaign'. The *Oxford English Dictionary* definition is 'an organized course of action to achieve a goal.' So there definitely has to be a goal (you'd be surprised!) and an organized course of actions (not easy, either) to that end. But great campaigns, as we are about to see, also possess real vision, ambition and inspiration. They display clarity of strategy and leadership. Often they require outstanding people. Always they are creative and innovative. Without astute and effective communications, however, few campaigns will be great.

But let's get one thing straight. The case studies featured herein are not just 'PR campaigns'. They are inevitably much broader than that. Indeed I will argue that all great campaigns are by definition integrated. Somewhat bizarrely, having spent the bulk of my career around the business, I have a major problem with the term 'PR'. And I'm not the only one. It is a strange little acronym and one that has been problematic for many decades. PR has overtures of manipulation and dishonesty. But more recently the term has been even more unhelpful because the art of communicating, or campaigning, has become so sophisticated in today's digital media.

It has meant that the 'PR' (what we would now describe as editorial persuasion or 'earned' media) has almost totally converged with other communications disciplines such as advertising and digital content marketing. Moreover, at a time of such intense scrutiny of public life, thanks largely to 24–7 rolling news and social media, it has become virtually impossible to exert long-term control via editorial media anyway. This is generally a good thing. It's good because it forces organizations and powerful individuals to be more transparent, more authentic. Yes, this book does confirm the demise of 'spin', but even 'PR', as most people know it, may itself be on a life-support machine.

PR's essential strengths, however, in holistic, rigorous, conversational communication, have become even more important to any successful campaign whether applied to political parties, corporations, individuals, brands or (rock) bands. Today we will see that great campaigns are more like conducting a well-tuned orchestra that combines all the instruments involved in paid-for, earned, owned and shared media communications. But while this book studies the evolution of public relations, it generally tries to avoid dry academic discussion. Instead, the narrative unfolds, warts and all, through a series of real-life examples.

So how could I draw some comparison between great campaigns across all those disciplines? I agonized over selection, eventually ending up with nine that I believe tell a diverse yet cohesive story. Three of these are political election campaigns (Margaret Thatcher, New Labour, Obama for America); one is more generally about surviving and thriving in public life (British Monarchy); two are more corporate and brand-focused (Dove's Campaign for Real Beauty and (RED)); two are grounded in sport (London 2012 Olympics and Brand Beckham); and one is pure entertainment (the Rolling Stones) albeit with much more besides. But the point is that such lines completely blur for all these campaigns. The best political efforts take some of their smartest thinking from the business world, and vice versa. David Beckham's incredible career is as much an entertainment and branding campaign as it is a sporting one. Yes, Product (RED) is a commercial campaign, but like Dove's Campaign for Real Beauty, it is heavily reliant on entertainment, popular culture and alliances with NGOs.

I have organized these case studies into three distinct themes, not necessarily in chronological order, because this helps narrate the evolution of the communications business from the mid-1970s to the present day. The first three (Thatcher, New Labour, Monarchy) are robust battles between politicians, public figures and the editorial media. This is the rough and tumble of public life – often red in tooth and claw – with adversity overcome and with sky-high stakes. In each case there is still, at least initially, an element of spin; an attempted manipulation of aggressive media. That said, they are also strategic, brave, innovative and effective, with much to be learned for anyone running a campaign today.

The second batch (Rolling Stones, Beckham, London 2012) are drawn more obviously from the worlds of entertainment and sport. Their success, while still heavily reliant on traditional PR, is also down to their efforts at building mutually profitable coalitions. There is still an element of overcoming adversity (as there is in any good narrative) but they are consistently optimistic and groundbreaking in their vision. They share a thick seam of inspiration and creativity.

The final tranche (Product (RED), Obama, Dove) brings us up to date. These very modern, highly digital campaigns take all the elements of the preceding chapters and reinvent them for a social media age. They also tell a fresh story about values-driven communications and purpose; now essential for a new generation of consumers and voters. Despite coming from different sectors (politics, NGOs and corporations), these campaigns could even be described as full-blown 'movements' at work.

In the final chapter I look at what we can learn from this selection of great campaigns. What are the qualities that unite them? What do we learn from them about effective communications? What do these campaigns tell us about how the media have evolved over this period? And what do they say about ourselves and our society? This summary will also examine the campaign stars themselves, and the sort of people and skills required to run great campaigns in the future. It will attempt to predict, based on all this intelligence, what the communications industry will look like in 2020 and beyond.

But let's start by stepping back in time to the fiery political climate of Britain in the mid-1970s ...

Part One
Old school, robust media battles but with leadership, strategy and innovation

Chapter One
Labour Isn't Working
The election of Margaret Thatcher – 1978–1979

Introduction

From a marketing and media perspective, Margaret Thatcher was the first truly modern British political leader and prime minister. Although she was prime minister for 11 years thanks to three general election victories, it was her 1979 election campaign that was the most groundbreaking. Moreover, it set the tone for her premiership and legacy.

Why the campaign shook the world

This campaign produced Britain's first (and so far, only) female prime minister. In 1979, when Margaret Thatcher was first elected, the swing away from the incumbent Labour government was 5.1 per cent, the greatest since Labour's Clement Attlee beat Winston Churchill at the end of World War Two.

It was to produce a startlingly new type of Conservative government: Thatcher was the first Conservative prime minister to come from outside the British 'establishment'. She offered genuine aspirational appeal to both Britain's middle and working classes. Significantly, her comms team comprised similarly non-establishment figures.

Lord Bell, 2015
Source Gavin Ellwood, Ellwood Atfield's gallery event, 24 March 2015 'How to Win (or Lose) an Election'

Thatcher went on to win the two subsequent elections (1983, 1987) on the same basic ticket. Lord Bell claims that Thatcher's election in 1979 'brought about the end of socialism, as we knew it, in Britain'. This may be somewhat hyperbolic but it is certainly true that Thatcher's leadership converted many in the opposition Labour movement into accepting the market dynamics of capitalism (and ultimately led to Tony Blair's 'Clause IV moment' – see Chapter 2).

Why is the campaign great?

This can claim to be Britain's first modern political campaign. Political communications was still a relatively new discipline in the 1970s. The 1960s had seen the end of the age of deference, from the media and public, towards the country's leaders. The proliferation of television sets with colour pictures in the mass market had led to rapid growth in the advertising industry. An increasingly pluralistic society encouraged a more open battle of ideas via the media and political system, which in turn encouraged rapid growth in the British PR industry.

Thatcher's election campaign openly embraced the brand marketing principles of the *Mad Men* era. It was innovative in applying visual, impactful advertising power to a British politician. As such the messages to the electorate were more emotional and populist than rational and highbrow. It was also the first highly-integrated political campaign, with the advertising and editorial communications knitted closely together under a single team.

The cast

Margaret Thatcher (1925–2013) – later Lady Thatcher
One of history's best-known and most controversial political figures. She was one of the few British prime ministers to have had a political movement named after them – 'Thatcherism'. The woman herself was an unusual blend of middle-class upbringing (a grocer's daughter from a market town in Lincolnshire, England), elite education (she read science at Oxford) and yet with a passion for many aristocratic

Baroness Margaret Thatcher, 2005
Source Allan House

institutions (the Monarchy, House of Lords). She was driven, focused and acutely aware of the need to communicate her vision in terms that the British public understood.

Gordon Reece (1929–2001), director of publicity –
later Sir Gordon Reece
Dapper and flamboyant in his style and lifestyle, Reece had been to a Catholic school and read law at Cambridge University but then decided to become a newspaper journalist. He later moved into television working on *This is Your Life* and *Emergency Ward 10*. Reece became close to the key newspaper editors of the 1970s including David English of the *Daily Mail* and Larry Lamb (the first editor of *The Sun* under its new owner, Rupert Murdoch). Reece met Thatcher when she was Shadow Education Secretary in the early 70s, when he was commissioned as a freelancer to produce a party political broadcast. Then during Thatcher's leadership campaign Reece made a famous promotional film of her carrying out domestic chores such as washing the dishes. After she had won the leadership, Thatcher made Reece her full-time adviser. He later went on to work with PR agency boss Peter Chadlington (later Lord Chadlington) on various City takeover deals.

Tim Bell, chief advertising executive and key adviser –
later Lord Bell

Bell was managing director of the Conservative Party's advertising agency Saatchi & Saatchi. He was to become Thatcher's personal adviser and ultimately one of her closest friends and confidants (see Campaign Star on p 13).

Other agency advisers from Saatchi & Saatchi

Margaret Thatcher actually had very few strategic political advisers in opposition, preferring to rely on external consultants. As well as Bell, this included the agency's co-founders **Maurice and Charles Saatchi,** creative director and key copywriter **Jeremy Sinclair** and account director **Bill Muirhead.** All continue to be involved in the agency that emerged from Saatchi & Saatchi in the 1990s, M&C Saatchi.

Ronald Millar (1919–1998), chief speechwriter

'Ronnie' Millar was Margaret Thatcher's main speechwriter from 1973 onwards. He was a former playwright and actor. Many of his speeches and lines went down in the political lexicon such as the famous statement: 'You turn if you want to. The lady's not for turning' which was a dual pun responding to accusations of making U-turns in policy and on the 1948 play *The Lady's Not for Burning* by Christopher Fry.

Party chairmen

These included **Peter Thorneycroft** (old-fashioned Etonian who was chairman during the 1978/79 election campaign and the man who originally agreed to hire Saatchi & Saatchi). He was later replaced by John Gummer, then by Chris Lawson (from Mars Petfoods), then Peter Brookes, then Norman Tebbitt.

Chris Patten, head of research – later Lord Patten

Patten, who was the party's head of research during the 1978/79 election campaign, went on to be secretary of state for education, governor of Hong Kong and chairman of the BBC Trust.

★ THE CAMPAIGN STAR ★
Tim Bell

Tim Bell may not have been directly employed by Margaret Thatcher during her crucial 1979 election campaign – he was the managing director of the Conservative Party's newly-hired ad agency Saatchi & Saatchi at the time – but he was nevertheless the pivotal figure and the one most trusted by Thatcher.

Born in 1941, Bell was a relatively youthful advertising executive at the time. Inspired by Thatcher and fiercely loyal, he was to learn quickly and soon became an adept and influential adviser. Despite being an 'ad man' in the early days, Bell also grasped the wider editorial process and forged strong relationships with key journalists and media owners. He realized he had an instinctive feel for how a narrative would play out in the short and long term.

Bell worked on all Thatcher's election campaigns but always as a consultant and via a number of different firms. He went on to set up his own agency, Bell Pottinger, with Piers Pottinger, which continues to be one of the UK's largest PR consultancies.

Bell is almost as divisive a figure in the comms business as his mentor Lady Thatcher was in the political world. He is forthright in his right-wing, libertarian views, which continue to offend many. This free-market approach has also extended to his consultancy work for politicians around the world, sometimes with questionable records on human rights.

Despite his controversial career which has included a selection of minor scandals, Bell inspires affection and loyalty among his clients and staff. Speak to alumni of Bell Pottinger and they talk of a man who always has time to advise on careers or help out with personal problems.

In person Bell is ever warm, charming and polite. Despite his political dogmatism he is lively company and a better listener than he gets credit for. He is also self-deprecating and candid once he trusts you. Surprisingly he has friends across the political spectrum.

In his 2014 memoirs *Right or Wrong*, Bell writes:

Margaret was an outsider – by sex, by upbringing, even in her largely non-collegiate approach – and in many ways she remained an outsider for many in the Tory Party. I was also an outsider; not public school, not even university. Certainly not establishment. In fact, I've been an outsider all my life and I've liked being so. When I started working for the Conservative Party (1978) I was an outsider because I came from the advertising industry – which to politicians in the 70s seemed like the rock music industry with added insanity. But I understood their world far better than they understood mine.

Despite starting as an outsider, Bell is now a life peer in the House of Lords, hugely wealthy and a genuine giant of the global PR industry. In his mid-70s he continues to go to the office every day, remains an all-round enthusiast and says he will 'never retire'.

Bell will go down as one of the pioneers of the modern corporate communications consultancy. His integrated approach to advertising and PR has become the norm in corporate and political marketing strategies. Few understand the convergence between business and geo-political interests like Bell. And he argues, with intellectual cogency, that everyone is entitled to commercial advocacy in the face of an increasingly aggressive media. This very argument has been central to the exponential growth of the PR industry since the 1980s.

★ ★ ★ ★ ★

THE CAMPAIGN

The context

The 1970s was an unsettled period in the sociology of Britain. The economy was struggling, there was growing racial tension following an influx of immigrants in previous decades, football hooliganism was rife, and powerful trade unions flexed their muscles via a series of crippling strikes. This backdrop created an existential crisis for the centre-right Conservative Party.

Historian Ewen Green claimed there was growing resentment among Tories of the inflation, taxation and constraints imposed by the Labour movement, which was associated with the so-called Buttskellite consensus (derived from the Conservative chancellor Rab Butler and Labour's Hugh Gaitskell) in the decades before Thatcher came to prominence.

Although the Conservative leadership tolerated the post-war Attlee Labour Government's reforms, there was continuous right-wing opposition from the lower ranks of the party. Among this group *The Road to Serfdom*, a book by the anti-socialist economist Friedrich von Hayek and later closely associated with Thatcherism, was gaining credence.

The previous general election in 1974 saw an uncharismatic soft-left Labour Party leader (Jim Callaghan) edge out an uncharismatic soft-right Tory prime minister (Edward Heath). In 1978 the economy was sluggish and the strikes continued, and yet opinion polls showed Labour in the lead with a general election expected later that year. Another Labour victory was becoming a serious possibility, which dismayed many in the Conservative Party and in the British media. A decade beforehand the aggressive entrepreneur Rupert Murdoch had entered the British newspaper market with his acquisition of the populist *News of the World*, followed in 1969 with the purchase of the struggling daily broadsheet *The Sun*. Murdoch converted *The Sun* into a tabloid format and reduced costs by using the same printing press for both newspapers. On acquiring it he

▶

appointed Albert 'Larry' Lamb as editor. Lamb later recalled that Murdoch had told him: 'I want a tearaway paper with lots of tits in it'. But Murdoch was also politically motivated, particularly in his opposition to what he saw as the overly-powerful British labour unions.

The objective

Margaret Thatcher was a winner. Despite being a woman from humble backgrounds, she had already defeated Edward Heath and Willie Whitelaw in the 1975 leadership election and was building momentum in the wider party. Thatcher was equally motivated by power and ideology. Her objective was a series of electoral victories, starting with the next one, in which she would transform Britain through her principles of greater personal freedom and national pride and by rolling back the power of the state.

The strategy

'There are only ever two campaign strategies in an election,' says Tim Bell. 'It's either the opposition saying "time for a change" or a government saying "the country's great again, don't let the other lot muck it up".' Thatcher's strategy was the former. It could be argued that the lack of sophistication by modern standards is precisely why this strategy pretty much ended once power had been achieved.

From the beginning Thatcher and her team were determined to emphasize dissatisfaction with the incumbent Labour administration and thus get the electorate to crave a modern Conservative alternative. They also realized that Thatcher – compared to previous leader Heath, current PM Jim Callaghan and indeed many other figures in British politics at the time – was a far more dynamic, exciting and aggressive personality.

How the narrative unfolded ...

Phase 1 *Thatcher finds her voice*

By 1978 Gordon Reece had already been the Tories' director of publicity for three years. This was an early incarnation of the political 'director of communications' roles we see today. He had been to the Republican Convention in the USA and studied the American political approach, including the case studies of Johnson and Nixon, and then the Carter versus Ford election in 1976. Tim Bell, who at the time was managing director of the Conservatives' ad agency Saatchi & Saatchi, says: 'Gordon clearly loved the glamour and salesmanship of it all. He recognized that the next British election would be a televisual contest – something that had proven very successful in securing the Australian Liberal Party's victory in 1975 – and that the campaign team needed to decide early on what the central campaigning issue should be.' Reece also recognized a left-wing bias to many core media at the time, both TV and press. He saw that on television shows Margaret Thatcher could come across as hostile and defensive. Hence he started switching his charge from appearing on the heavyweight political programmes to more populist shows.

Reece had begun work on Thatcher's image and especially how she looked and sounded on TV. Party political broadcasts before that time portrayed her as shrill and bossy, so Reece altered her hairstyle and wardrobe and, famously, took her for some voice coaching with legendary British actor Sir Laurence Olivier. Miraculously, she developed a warmer, husky tone.

This campaign began in earnest in 1978, however, with a speech to the Conservative Party conference in which Thatcher took a controversially strong line on immigration. She told that conference: 'It is true that Conservatives are going to cut the number of new immigrants coming into this country, and cut it substantially, because racial harmony is inseparable from control of the numbers coming in'.

Thatcher, unlike previous Tory leaders, was starting to strike a chord with the 'man on the street' and increasingly tailored her messages to dissatisfaction with what she saw as weak political leadership. As part of the radical message modernization process, Reece decided

Charles and Maurice Saatchi in the early days of Saatchi & Saatchi
Source M&C Saatchi

that he needed an advertising agency that was 'good at TV, up-and-coming and hungry for fame' according to Bell. Unsurprisingly Reece was pointed in the direction of Saatchi & Saatchi, which had been formed in 1970.

'Most of Saatchis probably voted Labour,' recalls Bell. 'So Maurice (the CEO) put me onto the account because I think he saw me as the Conservative on the payroll'. Bell was called to Thatcher's office. He recalls that on that first occasion she told him: 'If you have any tricks that will get me elected, don't use them. Because if the people don't want me, it won't work.' There is irony here because even though Thatcher was authentic, plenty of tricks were used in getting her elected.

Phase 2 *The new team's integrated approach*

The campaign team was now in place: a combination of Thatcher herself, chairman Lord Thorneycroft, Reece, Bell and head of research Chris Patten.

Although Britain's voting allegiance had always been divided along class lines, with the upper–middle (A/B) classes traditionally supporting the Tories and the working classes (D/E) supporting Labour, the team identified three core demographics that could swing the election in their favour: younger, first-time voters without blind party affiliation; skilled workers (C1/C2) who were fed up with industrial stagnation and unionization; and female voters who had tended in the past to vote Labour.

The British media were also politically aligned. And Bell saw the benefit in targeting those media with most sway among their target demographics. Bell explains: 'We wanted *Daily Mail* readers as ever, but we also needed readers of *The Sun*. The broadsheets would look after themselves. We always had in mind the Conservative Party campaign that ran in the late 1950s (from Colman Prentis and Varley, the first British ad agency to be hired by a political party) that showed workers such as milkmen and miners, with the line "I'm a Conservative".'

The mass-market newspaper *The Sun* had previously been a Labour-supporting journal and Larry Lamb was a working-class editor but he disliked the trade unions, particularly as their militancy was making it tougher to get the paper out each day. Bell says: 'Our media relations strategy centred on *The Sun*, and we got Larry Lamb to meet with Margaret on many an occasion, which finally convinced him – and in turn, Rupert Murdoch – to support us.'

The charming and persuasive Gordon Reece had already managed to bring many editors onside with the Thatcher project. Even Bob Edwards, director of the Labour-loyal Mirror Group, was said to like her. 'Being an outsider, a middle-class person with those values, Margaret treated journalists differently from previous Tory leaders,' explains Bell. 'She was the first political leader that talked to them. She had a drink with the editors. She knew them by name, and the same with the political correspondents. She wasn't at all grand with the media during the election.

'David English (*Daily Mail*) loved Margaret. We used to talk about how he could be supportive without being slavish. And Murdoch used to ask me: "what do you want in my papers?" It was because his political philosophy was identical to Margaret's. You couldn't get a cigarette paper between them. He was another example of a non-establishment, middle-class outsider.'

In this campaign the PR and the advertising were becoming seamless, with the same team responsible for both. Despite Thatcher's strong grasp of economics her team wanted an emotive, aspirational advertising campaign rather than delivering cold, rational arguments on economic policy that may turn voters off. This is why the single-minded, impressionistic advertising offered by Saatchi & Saatchi at the time was such a good fit.

Team Thatcher also yearned for 'event advertising' of the type that had been used in 1960s America. Democrat incumbent president Lyndon Johnson's team had used the powerful 'Daisy: Girl on the Hill' film in the 1964 election to attack his Republican rival Barry Goldwater. Goldwater reacted angrily, which created even more publicity for the film and the message therein. Johnson won the election. Bell says: 'We thought the holy grail was an ad that would be shown everywhere else as an event, that would capture the essence of the debate. I knew about this "event advertising" because Maurice Saatchi had studied books on the theory.'

And sure enough Saatchi & Saatchi came up with a classic. In August 1978 a giant 48-sheet poster was erected on just 20 outdoor sites across the country. It showed a long queue of unemployed people with the line 'Labour Isn't Working'. The photograph was actually faked using a group of Tory Party operatives and splicing them together to create a much longer queue. Bell recalls: 'Margaret's reaction when I showed her the artwork was "What's so clever about that?" But after a long conversation about it, she said it was "wonderful".'

When he saw the poster, Denis Healey, at the time Labour's chancellor, apparently went 'ballistic'. He accused the Tories of 'selling politics like soap powder' and called the poster 'phoney' because the 'unemployed' people pictured in the ad were actually employees. This created a major story in the media and soon most people in the country were aware of the poster, which has become one of the most famous political ads of all time.

'It was perfect because he had generated a huge news story,' says Bell. 'We never revealed who the people in the photograph really

Labour Isn't Working poster, 1978
Source Getty Images: The Conservative Party Archive/Contributor

were, and that just kept the controversy alive, to our advantage. From a spend of around £50,000 we ended up with a level of free media coverage that would normally have cost us millions if we'd bought all that space.'

He adds: 'Few people realize how much those creative craft skills transform the degree of impact that a political advert has. It was a big, bold poster. The newspaper editors were forced to physically go and look at the poster, which created an editorial impact in itself.'

Phase 3 *The election campaign begins in earnest*

Despite a by-now improving British economy, Prime Minister Callaghan surprised many by announcing on 7 September 1978 that there would be no general election for that year and he would wait until 1979 before going to the polls. The assumption was that he believed the economy could improve further, which in turn would improve Labour's electoral prospects. Either that or the Tories' aggressive advertising had seriously rattled Callaghan. Margaret Thatcher reacted to the announcement by branding the Labour Government 'chickens' and Liberal Party leader David Steel joined in, criticizing Labour for 'running scared'.

Thatcher's campaign team responded by ramping up the editorial pressure. In early January 1979 Callaghan attended a summit in Guadeloupe. The British media were critical of how little sleep the prime minister reportedly needed and Callaghan was branded 'sunny Jim' for admitting enjoying swimming in the Caribbean. When he returned from the trip the press were lying in wait at the airport. He was accused of complacency at a time when Britain was suffering another devastating wave of public-sector strikes, which became known as the 'winter of discontent' and the Soviet Union was posturing aggressively during the Cold War. Unwisely Callaghan, talking to an *Evening Standard* reporter at the airport, was dismissive of the mounting domestic chaos. Reece and Bell discussed this with Larry Lamb and together they came up with the headline 'Crisis? What crisis?' for Lamb's paper, *The Sun*. This front page became infamous both for summing up Callaghan's complacency and as a major turning point in the 1979 election campaign.

Soon afterwards Bell and his team came up with a fresh party political broadcast (PPB) for television. It is said that Thatcher favoured a direct confrontation with Callaghan while he was vulnerable, but Thorneycroft and Bell talked her out of it. Her team preferred to position their charge as a stateswoman and potential national leader, who was willing to take the high ground on the domestic crisis. The unions were, by implication, positioned as squabbling children, and the Labour Government their complacent teacher.

Written by Thatcher's chief speechwriter Ronnie Millar and head of research Chris Patten, the PPB contained lines such as 'This is no time to put party before country. I start from there' and 'In the national interest, surely government and opposition should make common cause ...'. 'This broadcast turned out to be one of the killer punches of the campaign,' claims Bell. 'We leapt to a 19-point lead in the opinion polls and Margaret's personal rating went to almost 50 per cent. I happen to think it won us the election.'

Early on in the campaign Reece and Bell had vetoed an election TV debate alongside Callaghan and (the Liberals' Jeremy) Thorpe, much to Thatcher's annoyance, because they were worried that she would come across as too aggressive. 'We feared she would tear Callaghan apart and people would view her as an arrogant bitch being disrespectful to a nice older avuncular figure,' Bell explains. The team was also keen for her to avoid any debates on health, education and social services, which they saw as Labour's natural strengths in public opinion. Thatcher actually resisted for a couple of months her team's pressure to push for a House of Commons vote of 'no confidence' in Labour's under-fire government. But then on 28 March 1979 she decided the time was right. Labour lost the vote and Parliament was dissolved.

In the run-up to polling day, Bell pushed to show once again the famous advertising poster and eventually the team agreed to use a slightly modified execution: 'Labour *Still* Isn't Working'. For television, the PR team set up a relentless series of photo-calls with Thatcher visiting rural and urban locations alike.

Bell explains: 'Our unbending belief was that we would win the election by communicating a *feeling* – be it of despair at Labour, or hope for a better future – rather than a rational argument'. This was a groundbreaking approach for political campaigning at the time.

On 4 May Margaret Thatcher and the Conservative Party won the general election with 339 seats out of a possible 635, giving the party a workable majority. They had gained 43.9 per cent of the popular vote.

The next day, speechwriter Millar came up with the St Francis of Assisi quotation in her victory speech: 'Where there is discord, may we bring harmony.' The speech was designed to position her as a stateswoman from the off, but ironically any harmony was to prove short-lived. Thatcher's first few years in government were to prove a tumultuous period in British history, with recession, union conflict and a war with Argentina.

Postscript ...

Despite being a political leader who went down in history for being strong (her dealings with the Soviet Union won her the nickname 'The Iron Lady'), abrasive and for dividing Britain ideologically, Thatcher's authenticity, political nous and communications skills were enough to win her another two elections (1983 and 1987).

'Margaret certainly believed, more than previous governments, that informing the public was important,' says Bell, who continued to remain an independent consultant – 'an outsider' in every sense – rather than a government spokesman. Bell and Reece came back to full-time strategic roles only when a general election was approaching. Bell went on, 'When I reflect on those days now we were a group of friends, rather than a tight professional team. We came back every four years for elections to be more strategic. The Conservative Party didn't choose their government comms people very well, tending to favour people who came from the privatized industries. They were 'no comment' merchants, whose main job was to handle the lobby. It's a problem with being in government; it makes you more and more remote.'

That said, Bell continued to advise Thatcher informally on her approach to key events, such as the Falklands War of 1982 and the miners' strike in 1984. And he was a key strategic force in the general elections. For the 1983 election the Conservative Party stuck with Saatchi & Saatchi, where Bell was still on the board. The advertising approach was 'Britain's on the right track, don't turn back.'

By the 1987 election Bell had left Saatchi & Saatchi and had formed Lowe Bell communications in conjunction with advertising man Frank Lowe. By now Bell was focusing more on PR than advertising. 'For 1987 Saatchis wanted a repeat of the "winter of discontent"-style work but we convinced Margaret to turn to Lowe Bell instead,' explains Bell. 'We used a series of pledges in that campaign – 400,000 more nurses and so on – it was a great campaign but she was so far ahead in the polls that it was an easy victory.'

In 1990 a challenge by Michael Heseltine, the Conservative Party's former secretary of state for trade & industry, eventually led to Thatcher's defeat in a party leadership election. She was forced to resign that autumn.

ON REFLECTION

- Almost every comms professional, leader or brand could learn from Thatcher and her team: in terms of authenticity and leadership, which are so often lacking in today's politics and business; in terms of the laser-like focus on certain issues and certain media; in terms of avoiding battles they knew they couldn't win; and in terms of the sheer determination, energy and creativity involved in this campaign.

- The 1978/79 campaign marked a coming of age for political advertising. This campaign was notable for the introduction of aggressive 'event' advertising to British politics. The idea was that certain ad executions could strike a nerve through insight, sharp copywriting and powerful imagery. Additionally, these 'attack ads' could create major controversy in the media, which would amplify the message via the ensuing editorial discussion.

- The campaign was both integrated, yet clear in its narrative. The campaign eschewed classic political campaign advertising, which tended to contain one single theme throughout, in favour of tactical executions on developing topical issues ('Labour Isn't Working').

- 'Labour Isn't Working' was witty at a time when most political advertising was boring and devoid of levity. Team Thatcher's ability to communicate 'a feeling' over and above the rational arguments for her election was also hugely significant. It all added to the sense of a popular movement for societal change.

- To be a harsh judge, Thatcher lacked real long-term strategy in her communications, particularly later in government, which left some feeling that she was making it up as she went along. Her priorities lurched from international conflict to smashing the unions, to the gradual and uneven privatization of state utilities.

- Nevertheless, the 1978/79 campaign became the model for every political election campaign that ensued. It was the first time anybody had ever communicated properly to the whole of the electorate and media, bearing in mind their demographics and preferences. As we will see in Chapter 2, it became an obsession of Tony Blair's to emulate Thatcher in this respect.

- For political marketers and communicators this is a difficult case study because, a third of a century on, the world has changed a great deal. Political parties had mass grassroots memberships at that point, unlike nowadays. In addition, the influence of the press has changed substantially, particularly with the proliferation of new digital, and arguably more democratic, media outlets. Hence the techniques used during team Thatcher's push for power are difficult to replicate via social media, which require a different communications approach (see the 'Obama for America' campaign, Chapter 8).

Acknowledgement

Right or Wrong (2014) Tim Bell, published by Bloomsbury Publishing

Chapter Two
New Labour, New Britain
Tony Blair's repositioning of the Labour Party – 1994–2005

Introduction

The campaign to totally reinvent Britain's centre-left Labour Party began in 1994 when Tony Blair was elected party leader following the death of John Smith. The campaign was so fundamental and ambitious in scope, however, that it is difficult to say when, or even whether, it ended. But there is little doubt that this was one of history's most disciplined and successful political campaigns, and one whose key players became legendary and notorious in equal measure.

Why the campaign shook the world

When Tony Blair took over in June 1994 the Labour Party – which was founded in 1900 – had already been out of power for 15 years. The party was still seriously divided internally having endured one of its most demoralizing election wipeouts (1983) and a previous general election (1992) where the media had denigrated and effectively destroyed the then leader, Neil Kinnock.

And yet less than three years after Blair took the reins, a rebranded, reinvigorated 'New Labour' was to claim a landslide election victory. Unlike many Labour Party election campaigns there was a strong emphasis on aspiration and hope. Even more incredibly, large sections of the previously Conservative Party-supporting press were to heartily endorse Blair. This landmark victory was followed by two further successes in 2001 and 2005 under the same leadership team. Blair remains the Labour Party's longest-ever serving prime minister. And he is the only Labour Party leader to have won a UK general election since 1974.

Tony Blair, 2009
Source Photo by Remy Steinegger, © World Economic Forum

But the repercussions weren't unanimously positive. Blair continues to divide opinion to this day – particularly after the controversial Iraq War, which began in 2003, and the lucrative business assignments he took on after leaving government. His media guru Alastair Campbell was similarly vilified in the media, both for shifting from power and policy in Westminster towards the media world, and for alleged manipulation of the media. Many in the Labour Party were, and still are, fiercely opposed to a modernizing campaign which they believe was quintessentially 'image over substance'.

Why is the campaign great?

The communications campaign set new standards in boldness and aggression. For a political campaign New Labour had unusual clarity in its objective and its strategy: to modernize the party, to win power and to modernize Britain. There was a young (Blair was 41 when he took over) single-minded leader and a group of modernizers from the same generation who both agreed with, and believed in, him. Blair's team subsequently displayed unity for the best part of a decade and almost military-style discipline in tactical execution of their campaign.

Alastair Campbell, New Labour's communications director, argues that the campaign was underpinned by constant innovation and a lack of complacency at any point, by zeal, unity and determination to win: 'Everybody who was part of it ... knew what we were trying to do. The aim was to win. The strategy was modernization, of the party and of Britain. Then the tactical stuff became easy, because everything was one of those two things. With New Labour, New Britain the narrative was always clear. From the beginning we wanted to modernize the party and scrap Clause IV. It was a question of building out from that.'

The New Labour campaign stayed remarkably consistent in approach and message for the first 10 years, with numerous opposition leaders foundering against its robust strategy and narrative. Tim Allan, who was Campbell's deputy, says, '"Labour is changing" was the narrative from the moment Tony became leader. Everybody

Tim Allan
Source *PRWeek*

could apply every story to that narrative. And then we could apply that to the country. We created meaning through difference. We were defining New Labour by not being Old Labour. Any great campaign is about semiotics. It's Saussure's [Ferdinand de Saussure – Swiss linguist and semiotician] theory: meaning is only created through difference.'

Like all great campaigns it was closely integrated – combining a powerful blend of policy, people, advertising, PR and design. And because of the scepticism of the British media at the time, this campaign was particularly characterized by the editorial (earned media) element taking precedence over the advertising.

While the advertising was creative and brave (albeit not to the degree of Saatchi & Saatchi's early work for Thatcher – see Chapter 1) the PR campaign was fundamental and groundbreaking. Political media chiefs had traditionally relied on serving Britain's aggressive pack of journalists, but New Labour's comms team sought equality.

Campbell and his team negotiated and battled with journalists, often even outflanked them.

Despite having to find their feet in a newly aggressive era of 24-hour rolling news, New Labour's press operation was always formidable; the team worked hard and fast, setting up rebuttal units to contest damaging stories. New Labour also introduced the concept of The Grid – a single-page guide within the strategic communications framework. It included a vertical column for each day, on which all the planned campaign activities for a given week were laid out. The Grid brought sharp coherence to a campaigning party or government alike. It enabled Campbell to keep track of what various ministers were doing and saying, enabling near dominance of the media agenda.

The cast

Whereas Britain's last great leader and communicator, Margaret Thatcher, had employed a more standard marketing communications 'client and consultancy' model (see Chapter 1), Blair opted to have his campaign gurus as fully paid-up members of the team.

The inner circle

If there was still a 'client' as such it was **Tony Blair** himself (effectively the operation's CEO) combined with his close partner, the shadow chancellor of the exchequer, **Gordon Brown** (effectively the chairman). Blair and Brown had long been friends and co-conspirators. Blair had convinced Brown to let him run unopposed for the 1994 leadership – a pact which later caused massive problems, indeed arguably led to the demise of the New Labour project 13 years hence.

Blair's main communications and strategy adviser, **Alastair Campbell**, was employed – similarly to Thatcher's Tim Bell – as the classic consultancy 'suit': the executive who oversaw the media campaign; who implemented the strategy; and who did his best to keep all parties onside. Starting as Blair's press secretary in 1994, Campbell became the prime minister's press secretary in 1997, and then director of communications and strategy from 2000 until 2003.

Former ad man, and now established Labour Party pollster, **Philip Gould** was the 'planner' who set the rigour behind the strategy, the voter insight and the data. But Gould was even more important than that. He was a creative force too, conjuring up Labour's new red rose logo, backdrops and imagery, as well as many of the key election phrases.

New 'red rose' logo, 1994
Source Jackie Stacey, on behalf of the Labour Party

Peter Mandelson was the party's former director of communications, who by 1992 was also a Member of Parliament. He was the 1997 campaign director and the mercurial and brilliant creative thinker in the team. Although Mandelson was the image mastermind in the early days, once in government he became distracted. Indeed he had to resign twice as a minister following separate scandals (1998 and 2001).

Other advisers

Beyond this core team, a much wider – but still formidably unified – group of people completed the New Labour project.

John Prescott, Blair's deputy leader from 1994, may not have been part of the strict inner circle but was essential to the leadership team and project, particularly in bringing the left-wing of the party onside with the centrist Blair.

There were also myriad non-politicians who were vital cogs in the operation. This group included Blair's chief of staff **Jonathan Powell**, chief speechwriter **Peter Hyman**, political assistant and 'gatekeeper' **Anji Hunter**, political secretary **Sally Morgan** and deputy press secretary **Tim Allan**.

Creatives

External advisers included **Chris Powell**, brother of Jonathan, who at the time was CEO of Labour's advertising agency BMP DDB. He was flanked by creative director **Pete Gatley**, who wrote many ads alongside BMP board director **Daryl Fielding** (see Chapter 9 on Dove's Campaign for Real Beauty).

TBWA's creative director **Trevor Beattie** was the influential creative behind the second and third election victories. Beattie – famous in the late 1990s for his Wonderbra 'Hello Boys' poster ads and the 'FCUK' work for French Connection – had worked informally with Peter Mandelson and the Labour Party since the mid-1980s. He said he had achieved his 'dream' when he officially won the Labour Party ad account in 2000.

Campbell says of this huge and impressive team: 'Tony didn't want to lose any of those brains. He also realized the value of non-politicos. Once there are too many politicians on a campaign team, there are too many agendas. So we ran a lot of the campaign from the leader's office. It was do-able because I was able to maintain a presence in all three camps – Tony's, Gordon's and John's.'

★ THE CAMPAIGN STAR ★
Alastair Campbell

New Labour boasted a tight team with some gifted communicators – not least Tony Blair himself and the media strategist-turned-MP Peter Mandelson – but if there was one pivotal communications genius throughout, it was Alastair Campbell.

Often described as 'the second most powerful figure in Britain' during this time, Campbell was central to, and arguably the most consistent force in, the New Labour project. From the moment (11 August 1994) when Blair talked the tabloid journalist into taking the role of press secretary, Campbell was his media minder, strategist and trusted confidant.

Campbell recalls that before hiring him Blair had confided: 'The job is called press secretary but it's much more than that. Tactical minds are two-a-penny but strategic minds are hard to come by, and you've got a strategic mind.' Along with strategic oversight, Campbell's focus on detail, soundbites and consistency of message was legendary. He even managed to transform the Labour Party's difficult relationship with the Murdoch-owned media.

In terms of British politics, Campbell's greater reliance on the media rather than Westminster to set national policy changed public life forever. Campbell had learned from the Conservatives' work with Thatcher in terms of controlling the image of their leader – an approach that was alien to many in the Labour Party. As such he became Britain's most notorious 'spin doctor'. For Britons Campbell tends to provoke admiration and contempt in equal measure, depending on one's political outlook. The unsavoury affair over the legitimacy of the Iraq War tarnished his reputation.

In person, Campbell is highly engaging – a big guy with a passion for politics, sport and business. He is also notable for his candour and self-knowledge. One can talk to Campbell about virtually any subject and he will reply with disarming honesty – even his own battles with depression and alcohol. A confident, classless demeanour enables him to engage with anyone, from world leader to working-class football fan. And yet Campbell, a dedicated supporter of Burnley FC, also tends to divide opinion because of his fierce, often tribal, loyalty. During his days as a tabloid journalist he was famous for once punching *Guardian* journalist Michael White when White made a joke about the untimely death of Campbell's former boss and media magnate Robert Maxwell.

Campbell seems more relaxed of late and he only has the occasional drink. He has written books about his depression and even three novels. His extensive political diaries are best-sellers and in 2015 published a book called *Winners: And how they succeed* which went straight to the top of the *Sunday Times* best-seller list for non-fiction.

THE CAMPAIGN

The context

The left in Britain was changing significantly in the early 1990s. A growing chunk of the party was influenced by former minister Anthony Crosland's *The Future of Socialism*, in which he outlined the need for traditional socialism to adapt to modern circumstances. Sociologist and Blair adviser Anthony Giddens had written about his take on *The Third Way* – a path between unbridled capitalism and communism – with a focus on social justice rather than equality. There was an important departure philosophically from the previous Labour Party focus on trade unionism, the state and the underprivileged.

The objective

There were three simple aims for Blair and his team: to win elections, to stay in power, to change the country.

The strategy

This is where the project was particularly strong and succinct. From early on, the strategy was party and national modernization, summed up in the four key words of the 1994 Labour Party Conference backdrop: 'New Labour, New Britain'.

new Labour
new Britain

Source Jackie Stacey, on behalf of the Labour Party

How the narrative unfolded ...

Phase 1   *Blair elected leader (June 1994) to the Labour Party Conference – October 1994*

Asked how and when the New Labour campaign truly began, Campbell replies: 'It started with policy, it started with the review of Clause IV.'

He is referring to what will go down in the public lexicon as 'the Clause IV moment' in the Labour Party's history. Blair was savvy enough to realize the power of a big symbolic philosophical event. Hence the first stage of Blair's political and communications exercise was to get the party to agree to change its very constitution: to accept the fundamental New Labour principle.

The looming deadline was the party's annual national conference in October at which Blair intended to launch a review of Clause IV, which traditionally sat at the heart of Labour's constitution. The clause committed the party to 'the common ownership of the means of production'; in other words nationalization of industry. Blair had privately told Campbell that he believed Clause IV 'committed the party to economic policies it no longer believed in, let alone pursued.'

However, on the day of Tony Blair's first speech as leader, when he intended to announce the review of Clause IV, there was still a sense of the massive risk involved with this moment. 'Even Tony and Peter were reluctant to have an actual mention of Clause IV in the speech itself,' recalls Campbell. 'It was John [Prescott] who said, "Look, if you're going to do it, don't bloody mess about, just do it." But I remember, on the morning of the conference, Tony saying to Peter: "What's the chance of us being dead in the water by tonight?" Tony and Peter were even concerned about my "New Labour, New Britain" backdrop. But, as it happened, there was barely a murmur. The truth is that everyone who elected TB as leader knew that it was the direction of travel and began to accept it.'

After this moment the team's confidence grew and the New Labour project hit full throttle (see Figure 2.1). 'I think the reason it became

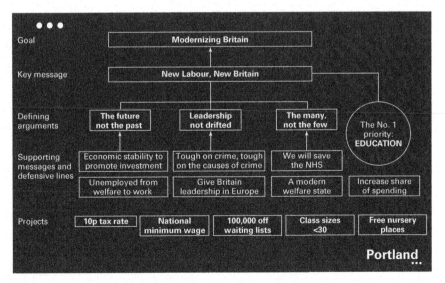

Figure 2.1 Labour's 1997 general election campaign messaging strategy
Source Portland Communications

a good comms campaign was because the media actually started looking for stories that fitted our message,' reflects Campbell. 'Before that first conference the stories were all "row over ..." or "anger as ..." but once we got through the Clause IV bit, the media thought: "Ah, this is serious and real." Even political editors like Philip Webster (*The Times*), Michael White (*The Guardian*) and Trevor Kavanagh (*The Sun*) got this basic message. And we stayed with this narrative throughout.'

Phase 2 *Getting New Labour into power – October 1994 to May 1997*

Campbell describes the next phase like this, 'The campaign message post-Clause IV was "you can trust us". Indeed the imperative for the New Labour team was to win over the highly sceptical British press. It faced two immensely powerful tabloids – *The Sun* and the *Daily Mail* – which had been Conservative-supporting since Margaret Thatcher's rise; the staunchly Conservative *Daily Telegraph*; *The Guardian*, which was the paper of Britain's liberal–left intelligentsia; and the working-class, Labour-supporting *Daily Mirror*.'

He goes on to recall, 'I remember talking to Tony when I first started working with him, and we were discussing what was the best result we could hope for. At that time the absolutely out-there target was maybe getting *The Sun* on board. But the basics were to try to stop *The Sun* and the *Daily Mail* killing us every day. We wanted the *Daily Telegraph* to take us seriously and the aim for *The Guardian* was to get it to accept the Labour Party saying the economy should be based around market principles. As for the *Mirror*, we just needed to keep them gung ho.'

What ensued was a tireless editorial offensive, with Campbell, his deputy Tim Allan and their colleagues relentlessly churning out stories, opinion–editorial pieces, photocalls and charm offensives for the media, especially the centre-right press.

Allan says, 'We worked incredibly hard at producing copy. Alastair, as a tabloid journo, could produce articles very quickly. And let's not forget that this new, young, dynamic leader Tony Blair was hot property. So we produced literally hundreds of opinion articles by Tony, as well as from other shadow ministers like David Blunkett. It enabled us to dominate the media agenda for three years or so, before the media got bored with this.'

Differing significantly from the Thatcher campaign of 1979, New Labour's media strategy was press-led. Campbell and Allan were noticing that by changing the attitudes of previously antithetical newspapers, the broadcast media were beginning to take note of the phenomenon. Allan explains: 'The value of a positive piece in, say, the *Daily Mail* was also that other papers were interested in the very fact that Labour could now get such a piece in the *Mail*. This became an essential part of the Labour narrative of change.'

New Labour's biggest media victory however – and a uniting theme of successful British election campaigns for decades – was the change of heart in Rupert Murdoch's News International, which owned *The Sun* and its Sunday equivalent the *News of the World*. In 1995 Blair and his team flew halfway around the world to Hayman Island off the coast of Australia, where they addressed Murdoch and a conference involving the leaders of his global News Corporation, laying the groundwork for Murdoch's eventual support of New Labour in British parliamentary elections.

Campbell says: 'I think even the visit to Hayman Island, which we knew was controversial and would be portrayed as us licking Murdoch's boots, showed a sense of boldness to the party and other media. We took a lot of flak. And yet in a funny way, the more flak we took the better it was. It also unsettled the opposition.'

Campbell and his team were regularly criticized at the time for bullying individual journalists. But Campbell counters: 'The whole bullying of the press thing was overblown. Yes, we negotiated – and there was a swing back towards the PR operatives – but the British media couldn't really be bullied.'

Simultaneously, the New Labour team was also gradually developing a power approach to advertising. As the 1997 election drew closer, Campbell had to take paid-for media more seriously. 'We tried to make the campaign genuinely integrated,' says Campbell, 'Eventually you couldn't really separate the PR and the advertising. But it wasn't an easy birth. We had a lot of trouble with our advertising agency [BMP DDB] in the early days. Daryl Fielding [BMP board director] found us impossible. And I don't blame her. There were some terrible tactical posters at the beginning. Eventually there was a guy called Pete Gatley [BMP creative director] who was very temperamental and emotional but we really got on. There came a point where he and I went off on our own and did the election stuff together.'

Perhaps because of its aggressive PR stance, New Labour's advertising is often remembered for certain attack ads. But Campbell insists the approach was roughly three positive ads for each negative execution: 'The truth is that the negative advertising, which Tony personally didn't like, was really aimed at the media at this time, whereas the positive ads were aimed at the electorate. Although the negative posters created a lot of journalist interest, we wanted positive messages out on the streets'.

The more positive ad executions, designed by Gatley, mirrored New Labour's famous 'pledge card' to the electorate, in which Blair

New Labour poster, 1997
Source BMP DDB

laid out key aspects of Labour's manifesto in colourful fonts. Later there was a poster featuring a 1997 Lord Snowdon portrait of a young-looking Blair with the optimistic tagline: 'Because Britain deserves better' (see previous page).

It was the attack ads that became notorious, however, particularly because of Chris Powell's smart media buying. Campbell recalls: 'There was a great one we did on that big revolving light space on Piccadilly Circus entitled "22 Tory tax rises". It wasn't up long but it generated a page in the news section of the *Evening Standard* and [BBC's TV programme] *Newsnight* showed it that night.' Even more controversially, there was a campaign that never went ahead featuring (incumbent Conservative prime minister) John Major as derogatory 'Mr Men' characters including 'Mr Weak' and 'Mr Dither' but which still got picked up by some media.

By spring 1997 all the momentum had shifted to New Labour. This culminated, on 18 March, in *The Sun* telling its readers to vote Labour, switching sides after more than 20 years of unswerving support for the Conservative Party. In a front-page article headlined 'The Sun Backs Blair' the paper, with a daily readership of over 10 million, wrote than Blair should be the next prime minister because he was 'the breath of fresh air that Britain needed'. It described the Tories as 'tired, divided and rudderless' and no longer deserving of support.

Only five years earlier the paper had claimed it was 'The Sun wot won it' for John Major in the 1992 election. How times had changed. During that previous campaign *The Sun* had run a personal and vitriolic attack against Labour's former leader Neil Kinnock, culminating in a front page that superimposed his head on a lightbulb with the headline: 'If Kinnock wins today will the last person to leave Britain please turn out the lights'. Nevertheless Campbell stresses: 'We didn't win because they [News International] backed us. They backed us because we were clearly going to win.'

In the weeks running up to polling day, and following a formidable effort by the New Labour comms team, a cascade of media and celebrities came out in support of Blair. In May, Labour won 419 seats in Parliament – a record for a Labour Government. It also won 42.3 per cent of the votes cast – Labour's best performance since 1966.

Phase 3 *In power at last, and focusing on winning a second term – 1997 to 2001*

Campbell describes himself and Tony Blair feeling 'flat' immediately following this landslide victory. One senses this is the nature of both beasts – natural 'winners' tend to quickly move on to the next challenge – and because their real campaign had only just begun with massive tasks ahead; not least the transition from opposition to government.

Campbell says: 'Once we'd won the election the campaign emphasis immediately shifted from New Labour to New Britain. The communications was now built around the question: what does New Britain feel like for the media and the electorate? But the overall narrative remained largely the same.'

Campbell shifted his role to become chief press secretary in Number 10 Downing Street, Tim Allan to special adviser in the press office. The duo noticed an immediate change in the attitude of the media, who now expected a more traditional approach to ensue. They were to be disappointed. The New Labour comms team maintained their aggressive and single-minded strategy to progressive modernization. Campbell recalls: 'I used to love it when I saw the press rolling their eyes in the Number 10 briefings. It was because they were realizing they had to do the same stories all over again. It just showed the consistency of our narrative.'

Allan adds, 'This is what sums up a great PR campaign: the difference between narrative and message. You don't have to worry about the message of each story because the overarching narrative remains clear. Journalists start doing it for you. I think we had a ridiculously long honeymoon period in government because the media were buying into our narrative. Even stories about the politicization of Whitehall suggested things had changed. Even the bad stories were ventilating our core message.'

That said, within a few months of their election win, the Blair Government was hit with its first media crisis – when rumours emerged of a deal with Formula One (F1) boss Bernie Ecclestone to postpone Labour's manifesto commitment to ban tobacco advertising, on which F1 was heavily reliant. Ecclestone had donated £1 million to the Labour Party under Blair. Speaking on BBC1's *On the Record* programme in November 1997, Blair put up a robust media defence against any suggestions of impropriety, saying he had been 'hurt and upset' by much that had been written about him. 'I think most people who have dealt with me think I am a pretty straight sort of guy, and I am,' he said. The quote became legendary. 'That period was when our inexperience really came through,' admits Allan, 'because dealing with a government story was very different from dealing with an opposition story.'

Despite a handful of crises during their first term, the New Labour project was progressing well and the team was already gearing up towards the next general election. By 2000 Mandelson, Campbell and Gould were looking to revive the party's advertising approach and hired the TBWA agency, led by maverick creative director Trevor Beattie. At the time, in *Marketing* magazine, Beattie said he thought the previous election campaign had been 'too low key, quite gentle' and set about creating an edgier strategy. Campbell says of Beattie: 'Trevor had been around us for years and was always supportive. But for the second election he really became the main guy. He had good people with him. He wanted to get to the guts of what we were about.'

The fresh advertising approach was to be epitomized by a poster showing the Conservative Party's new leader, William Hague, pictured wearing a Margaret Thatcher-style wig with the tagline 'Be afraid. Be very afraid.' The message being that the Conservative Party hadn't changed as it claimed, and was still in thrall to the right-wing legacy of Thatcher. 'That was the best ad,' smiles Campbell. 'Trevor had had it in his bottom drawer for ages and showed it to me but didn't want to stop his team coming up with other ideas. The original strapline was "Vote Labour on Thursday. Or this gets in", but we changed it to tone it down. Tony didn't like it at first, then after a while he laughed. And I said "but that's why it's great; it makes people laugh but makes a serious point".'

In May 2001 Labour once again won an impressive victory – 413 seats, just six fewer than in 1997, and the party polled 40.7 per cent of the popular vote. It was later described by media as 'the quiet landslide'.

Phase 4 *Second and third terms in office – and Blair eventually steps aside – 2001 to 2007*

A policy priority for New Labour's second term was an attempt to modernize and improve Britain's schools and hospitals and the communications emphasis shifted accordingly. The team also had to deal with the controversial decision, for a socialist party, of increasingly drafting in the private sector to help. This drew criticism from many within the Labour movement too, some of whom believed the party was moving too far to the right.

Campbell says: 'The media went for this story about the public reform agenda. It was controversial. But we were happy about this. The campaign still felt like New Labour. The fact that our key party communicators complained about the "repetition" of messages showed me that we were still on track.'

However, the New Labour project became seriously sidetracked by the 9/11 attacks in 2001 and the subsequent wars in Afghanistan and Iraq. Criticism was building of Blair's 'unhealthy' closeness to President Bush in the United States.

In the run-up to the Iraq War in 2003 Campbell himself was involved in the preparation and release of the 'September Dossier' (September 2002) and the 'Iraq Dossier' (February 2003 – later branded 'the Dodgy Dossier'), both of which argued the case for action over the presence of weapons of mass destruction in Saddam Hussein's Iraq. Both were alleged to have overstated the findings of military intelligence and for the latter Campbell was accused of 'sexing up' the document to be consistent with President Bush's aggressive policy towards Iraq. Campbell's subsequent battles with the BBC, which came to a head in the Hutton Inquiry (August 2003) into the death of former weapons inspector David Kelly, led Campbell to resign his role. Although Hutton cleared the Government of wrongdoing, Campbell had unfortunately 'become the story'.

There was equally renewed conflict within Labour's ranks, which was heavily reported in the media, and Campbell – who returned to help with the forthcoming election campaign – concedes that 'the tribe was beginning to fall apart'. Even New Labour's iron discipline in communications appeared to be softening. There was a sub-current of a different agenda emerging in the media that Brown, naturally further to the left than Blair in his political philosophy, was unhappy with certain policies. It was reported that Brown's personal spin doctor Charlie Whelan was briefing against Blair in the media, and possibly even Brown himself.

Unfortunately, this increasingly public battle within New Labour again hijacked the narrative the team was trying to maintain. Allan admits internal divisions were damaging the wider campaign: 'Most people knew there was this animosity, but by now the big change was that certain people, like Gordon, started to define themselves by not being New Labour.' Brown's gradual distancing from the New Labour campaign was symbolized by a powerful speech to the party conference in autumn 2003, when he ended with the line: 'This Labour Party – best when we are boldest, best when we are united, best when we are Labour.' Despite the growing internal divisions and less energetic campaign, Labour won the election in 2005, albeit with a much reduced number of seats: 356 and with just 35.3 per cent of the popular vote.

'By 2005 even trying to get Tony and Gordon to play on the same pitch was pretty grim,' says Campbell. 'Later that year myself and Philip [Gould] went up to St Andrews during a summit and said to Tony: "Look, if you're keeping Gordon as chancellor and the economy is centre-stage, you're going to have to work together, and you're going to have to signal that this is your last go".' What Campbell meant was that Blair's 1994 pact with Gordon Brown – that he would eventually step aside and let his rival lead – was now looking well overdue. 'Was I right or wrong to do that?' muses Campbell. 'To this day I'm not sure.'

By now Brown was openly briefing the media that Blair had gone too far on certain policies and was forming his own alliances with newspaper editors. 'Gordon started dealing directly with Paul Dacre (editor of the *Daily Mail*). It was really hard for us,' says Campbell. 'The media knew the poison in the Blair–Brown relationship but we had to pretend it wasn't happening. By now journalists were rolling their eyes for other reasons when we were briefing them on a cabinet meeting. I always operated on the basis that everything was on the record, but Whelan was briefing separately that Brown had stormed out or something.'

The media and political pressure continued to mount on Blair. He had been in power for 10 years and some commentators argued he had become too 'presidential', allowing hubris to affect his judgement. In June 2007 Blair resigned. At the end of his final Prime Minister's Questions in the House of Commons he received an unprecedented standing ovation from MPs from all sides. Gordon Brown took over as prime minister, with a determination to stamp his own authority on the party and to reintroduce some of the more traditional Labour policies. It could be argued that the New Labour campaign effectively ended that day.

Postscript ...

In September 2009, on the eve of the Labour Party conference, and seven months before the next general election, *The Sun* announced with a front-page editorial that it was turning its back on Labour after more than a decade of support. Instead it was throwing its weight behind the Conservative Party led by David Cameron, a politician who was known to have admired Blair. The headline read: 'Labour's Lost It'. And indeed in May 2010 the Labour Party under Brown achieved just 29.1 per cent of the popular vote. It had fallen well short of winning a majority of seats. Labour lost power to a coalition of the Conservative and Liberal Democrat parties. The next party leader, Ed Miliband, was to further disown 'New Labour', but slumped to a major defeat in the 2015 general election with around 30 per cent of the vote, and resigned.

ON REFLECTION

- New Labour was an unusual political campaign in that the leadership's ideology was defined by its difference from the party's previous ideology. It was deliberately rolling away from the damaging perception of the past. The campaign had that classic 'challenger brand' positioning: 'change'.

- Much of the success of this campaign was down to Tony Blair himself, one of the most natural communicators ever to grace politics. But Blair was smart enough to recognize his shortcomings and surround himself with more objective professional communicators such as Mandelson, Gould, Campbell and Allan. In marketing and communications terms it felt like the perfect client–agency relationship.

- New Labour applied the product marketing terminology of 'new' to what was a 100-year-old political party of the working class. All PR, advertising, design, music was geared around this premise. Few could claim that they didn't know what New Labour stood for, which is ironic considering its lack of purist ideology.

- Underpinning the campaign was a drive to restore mass membership of the party, leading to a peak of almost 500,000 in 1997, a figure last seen in the late 1970s. This gave the sense of a movement. And when Blair walked into Downing Street in May 1997, it felt like a moment in history.

- There were the essential elements of aspiration and hope in the 1997 election campaign, as epitomized by the official New Labour song in 1997: 'Things can only get better'. Many Labour Party campaigns since have lacked these.

- New Labour's strategists realized that, with a naturally conservative media establishment, they needed to be aggressive and permanently on the front foot. Very few parties anywhere today operate without something similar to New Labour's 'grid' system of media operations. New Labour's instant rebuttal units, designed to quickly refute negative allegations, have become commonplace around the world.

- All that said, the decision to go to war in Iraq was particularly damaging reputationally for both Blair and Campbell. For some, Blair will always be perceived as a liar (over the never-discovered 'weapons of mass destruction') and someone who placed too much priority on his loyalty to President Bush. While Campbell's alleged 'dodgy dossier', which he used to justify the 'weapons of mass destruction' claims, made him become a negative national story in his own right. It undermined his strategic power and a sizeable chunk of the Labour Party mistrusted the New Labour leadership from then onwards.

- Nevertheless, few would deny that New Labour, New Britain goes down in history as an inspiring, innovative and highly effective campaign – one in which modern marketing communications techniques were applied successfully to a previously divided and struggling party.

Acknowledgement

Winners: And how they succeed (2015) Alastair Campbell, published by Hutchinson, Random House

Chapter Three
A right royal renaissance
Rescuing the British Monarchy – 1997–2011

Introduction

The renaissance in the British Monarchy's reputation after the death of Princess Diana was both hard fought and remarkably successful. It had repercussions for any national public institution in any country, for the media, and for communications professionals around the world. This long-running campaign secured the Monarchy's future for a generation despite a torrid state of affairs when a new cohort of advisers was first called in.

Why the campaign shook the world

Between 1992 and 1997 the British Monarchy encountered its biggest crisis since the abdication of Edward VIII in 1936. As the age of deference was coming to an end, and with an increasingly aggressive and intrusive British media, a string of damaging stories about the private lives of the royals created a narrative more akin to a downmarket soap opera than a venerable institution. A once senior adviser to the family now recalls: 'People began to question what the Monarchy was for'. The slump in popularity, in stark contrast to the

Paddy Harverson, 2015
Source Julian Dodd

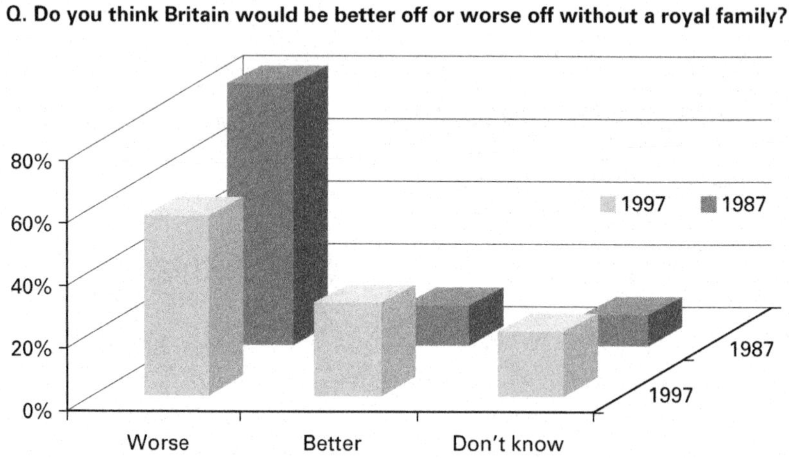
Q. Do you think Britain would be better off or worse off without a royal family?
80%
60%
40%
20%
0%
1997
1987
1987
1997
Worse
Better
Don't know

Figure 3.1 The popularity of the royal family in Britain had slumped dramatically in 10 years
Source ICM/*Guardian*

widely acclaimed wedding of Prince Charles to Lady Diana Spencer in 1981, came to a head in September 1997 immediately following the death of Diana. The royal family's response to her death was perceived to be 'cold' and 'out of touch', creating a crisis of public confidence (see Figure 3.1).

However, the campaign of modernization and professionalism that ensued over the next decade was to have an astounding effect. The reputation of the family, particularly the heir to the throne, had improved considerably by 2008. Three years later another royal wedding, this time involving Prince William and Kate Middleton, was deemed a global PR triumph. By then talk of republicanism, so rife during the 1990s, was largely off the British political and media agenda.

The campaign also shook the world because it unwittingly uncovered the practice of British tabloid newspapers hacking into the phones of figures in public life, which was to have long-term repercussions for public trust in media, politicians and some PR professionals (see phone-hacking scandal on p 71).

Why is the campaign great?

This campaign, which began in earnest in 1997, was an example of how a professional communications strategy could impact on even a traditionally closed institution such as Britain's royal family. It was an illustration of how disciplined and rigorous media relations and planning were by now essential in an era of 24-7 rolling news, where media scrutiny had heightened.

In the early stages, this campaign was characterized by an aggressive approach towards the press, arguably necessary at first but to the Monarchy's detriment. In the latter stages, however, the campaign used broadcast media plays and inspired photography to transform the family's image, and ultimately even embraced social media to capitalize on a more useful, transparent and sympathetic public narrative.

Nevertheless, there is a sense that maybe the Monarchy went too far in bringing the media to heel, without establishing mutual trust, which may be storing up problems in the future.

The cast

Prince Charles (born 1948), **Prince William** (born 1982),
Prince Harry (born 1984), the other 'directors of the firm'
based at Clarence House

Prince Charles, as heir to the throne, was a central player in this campaign and the member of the royal family suffering the most acute reputational woes during the 1990s and beyond. It was Charles and key members of his staff who drove the campaign in the early days. Despite running a separate royal household, Clarence House, Charles increasingly worked closely with the Queen and Buckingham Palace to pursue a wider strategy of modernization and professionalism. He has always mistrusted the media but has now learned to work better with them. Increasingly it is his sons, William and Harry, who are inheriting his mantle (and developing their own style). And while they may have learned a new media approach, they may also have inherited their father's mistrust of the press.

Camilla Parker Bowles, née Shand (born 1947) –
later the Duchess of Cornwall

Camilla worked closely with her husband-to-be, Charles, and Clarence House to rehabilitate his reputation and establish herself as acceptable to the public. She was arguably the first commoner to marry into the royal family as a mature and fully-formed media operator. Advisers say that Camilla, unlike many other royals, actually likes journalists and has a natural affinity with them. Although she never gives interviews, Camilla is smart enough to take advantage of media opportunities that arise and to use charm offensives when necessary, such as during the staged first appearance with Charles as 'a couple' outside London's Ritz Hotel.

HM Queen Elizabeth II (born 1926), effectively the firm's major shareholder, based at Buckingham Palace

At the time of writing Queen Elizabeth II was set to become the longest-serving monarch in British history, overtaking her great-great-grandmother Queen Victoria. Occupying the throne since 1952, Elizabeth has overseen a wider campaign that effectively secured the future of the British Monarchy for at least the next generation. She has always pursued an overall strategy that sets the royal family apart from politics, which the rest of her family has largely followed since, ultimately saving its reputation. Former courtiers attest to Elizabeth's determination and adherence to a 'set of values' which provide the foundations for this 'royal renaissance' campaign. It is her decisions, personal appointments and consistency in approach that underlie this campaign. And advisers attest to her calm and consistent leadership with an eye on wider media trends.

Sir Michael Peat (born 1949), effectively finance director/ managing director – knighted in 1998

Outside the royal family itself, Sir Michael Peat is the executive who most consistently drove the campaign to 'privatize and modernize' the British Monarchy during this period. Paddy Harverson, whom Peat hired as Clarence House's first director of communications in 2004, describes Peat as 'the cleverest guy I ever worked with'. He is great-grandson of William Barclay Peat, founder of the accountancy firm KPMG. Peat was educated at Eton College and at Trinity College, Oxford and joined the 'family' accountancy firm in 1972, becoming a partner in 1985. As such Peat led a 1986 study into the financial management of the royal household and for the next two decades was a key auditor of the Privy Purse and administrative adviser to the royal household. Significantly, Peat, working with the then Lord Chamberlain David Airlie, made a report with 188 recommendations to modernize the royal household. One adviser describes the plan, which is still referred to today, as the drive 'to take back our own destiny from the government and to do that we had to have control over the finances, a proper management structure, and then recruit people who were more in tune with the modern way of life'. As a result of this report Peat, in 1996, took up an official role with the royal household, where he became treasurer to the Queen, and then from 2002 to 2011 was the principal private secretary to Charles, Prince of Wales and Camilla, Duchess of Cornwall. At Clarence House he became absolutely pivotal in the campaign to rescue the Monarchy's image.

Mark Bolland (born 1966), deputy private secretary to the Prince of Wales, 1996 to 2002

Mark Bolland was an unusual appointment for Clarence House at the time. He was a relatively young, openly gay, comprehensive-school-educated marketing executive. Bolland, who was quickly branded 'Blackadder' after the manipulative Rowan Atkinson TV character, was the first dedicated 'spin doctor' to be hired by the royal family. Bolland is the long-term partner of Guy Black who ran the Press Complaints Commission at a crucial time in this campaign, a tie-up that was to prove important in improving, at least temporarily, Clarence House's relationship with the media. Bolland certainly set about changing the rules for press engagement with gusto and verve. For many within the media, and even in parts of the royal family, Bolland was seen as a divisive and manipulative character. Controversially after leaving Clarence House he went on, in 2003, to write the 'Blackadder' column in a tabloid newspaper, which was scathing about many royals. Nevertheless, history may show that he was the true catalyst for change in the Monarchy's media strategy. And he was certainly responsible for re-introducing Camilla Parker Bowles to British public life. In 2001 the PR industry bible *PRWeek* gave Bolland the 'PR Professional of the Year' award for his work on 'the public repositioning of Charles and Camilla'.

★ THE CAMPAIGN STAR ★
Paddy Harverson

Patrick 'Paddy' Harverson – later LVO – was communications secretary to the Prince of Wales (Charles) and the Duchess of Cornwall (Camilla) from February 2004 in addition to being official spokesman to the Duke and Duchess of Cambridge (William and Kate).

Harverson was born in 1962 and earned his degree at the London School of Economics (LSE). He served as a journalist on the *Financial Times* newspaper from 1988 to 2000. He had started as a stock market reporter, moved to New York correspondent, and ended up as sports correspondent from 1997 to 2000. He then joined Manchester United football club as its first director of communications, working closely with legendary head coach Sir Alex Ferguson. Harverson joined the office of the Prince of Wales at Clarence House in February 2004 for a rumoured £130,000 per year.

When Harverson had his leaving party at the end of Manchester United's employment, he was presented with a video message from Ferguson himself. Sir Alex couldn't be there as he was in Dubai with the players. But he did want to offer his best wishes to the young media star and thank him for steering the club through some testing times with aplomb. Harverson recalls: 'When I first told Sir Alex I was leaving Manchester United for Clarence House he said: "Son, you're going to the only place madder than this".' As is tradition in journalism and PR, his colleagues mocked up a 'leaving newspaper'. On the back page there was a classic headline from his time at United: 'Ferguson versus Wenger: This is War', and on the front page a recent tabloid headline: 'Prince Charles: I am not a murderer.' Indeed the media at the time also drew comparisons between Ferguson and his new boss, Prince Charles. Both were national icons and both had reputations for being autocratic and temperamental. *The Guardian*, writing at the time of Harverson's appointment, said that perhaps Prince Charles, who had hand-picked him, was hoping 'that some of the success of one of the world's most successful sporting empires may yet rub off on a somewhat tarnished royal household'.

It commented that 'anyone who can handle David Beckham's profile and Sir Alex's hubris, should find the royal princes' love lives, not to mention their father's, relatively straightforward.'

Today Harverson says: 'There were some similarities between working for Manchester United and the royal family. Both were national institutions in which there was relentless media interest. And in both cases there was an extraordinary imbalance between the demand for, and supply of, access to the principals.' But whereas Ferguson had long used the media as a tool, there was still the residue of the age-old 'never complain, never explain' approach when Harverson joined the royals in 2004.

To many, Paddy Harverson was naturally more 'establishment' than his predecessor, Mark Bolland, and he quickly employed a more straightforward approach. One royal correspondent at the time describes Harverson as 'No nonsense. Absolutely as straight as a die'. Some journalists claimed he had a tendency to 'over-react' to negative stories and lacked subtlety. One, using a football analogy, even said he was 'prone to a two-footed tackle'. But Harverson is keen to point out that he was deliberately robust with the media at the time to reassure the young princes that they were protected.

There is little doubt that Harverson was the media strategist who completed the renaissance of Prince Charles and the wider royal family. Credited with masterminding the global coverage of the successful 2011 royal wedding between Prince William and Kate Middleton, Harverson was honoured by *PRWeek* that October as 'PR Professional of the Year'.

In person Paddy Harverson is broad, stands well over 6ft tall, has a shaven head and well-groomed beard. Quite apart from his physical stature, he possesses a quiet natural authority and gravitas that make people listen and respect him. And while he undoubtedly has the ability to be robust, he is more naturally thoughtful and laid back.

At the time of writing he co-runs a 'discreet' corporate PR consultancy called Milltown Partners, with former Google PR boss D-J Collins, which is fast expanding after just two years.

★ ★ ★ ★ ★

THE CAMPAIGN

The context

The 1990s were to prove a torrid time for the reputation of the British Monarchy. After a period of relative stability and some popular royal weddings, which the media lapped up, the private lives of many of the royal family had become riven with marital crises and minor scandals.

For the Queen the personal nadir was probably 1992, which she famously described as her 'annus horribilis'. That year Andrew Morton's book, *Diana: Her True Story* placed Prince Charles's troubled personal life in global focus; Princess Anne had divorced her husband Mark Phillips; and Prince Andrew separated from his wife Sarah Ferguson. Then, just to complete a classic 'soap opera' storyline, there was a major fire at the Queen's home, Windsor Castle, causing devastating damage. Perhaps unsurprisingly, considering the growing public disillusionment, there followed political and media outcry over whether the public purse could be used to pay for repairs at Windsor.

Between 1992 and 1997 the Queen had sought to revive the family with the help of modernizing adviser David Airlie, the Lord Chamberlain. Airlie set up the Lord Chamberlain's committee made up of external advisers, which still exists today. But progress was slow owing to a fundamental debate between the new wave of modernizers and more traditional resisters to change. Even before Diana's death in August 1997 a *Guardian*/ICM poll found that only 48 per cent of those polled thought the country would be worse off without the Crown, an historically low proportion.

From her engagement to the Prince of Wales in 1981 until her death in 1997, Diana Spencer had become a major presence on the world stage. She was often described as 'the world's most photographed woman'. She also built a reputation for her style, charisma and high-profile charity work, in contrast to her difficult marriage to the Prince of Wales. Immediately after her death Prime Minister Tony Blair accurately described her as 'the people's princess'. But

Prince Charles and Diana had divorced in 1996. Worse, Diana had been publicly critical of the way Charles had treated her during the marriage. In a BBC *Panorama* interview in November 1996 she said: 'My husband made me feel inadequate in every possible way that each time I came up for air he pushed me down again ...'.

When Diana was killed in August 1997 in her chauffeured car in Paris, while being chased by a pack of journalists, it sent a profound shock through the institution. In the aftermath of Diana's death, the Queen and other members of the royal family were perceived in the tabloid press as reacting in a cold and unfeeling way because they had failed immediately to participate in the public outpouring of grief. The Queen was accused by some of a failure to capture the mood of the nation, in stark contrast to the media-savvy new Prime Minister Blair.

Public and media anger began as a result of the decision to issue a 'business-as-usual' message by taking princes William and Harry to church at Balmoral only a few hours after Charles had broken the news to them of their mother's death.

The Queen was criticized for remaining in Scotland too long rather than returning to London, where mountains of flowers had been placed by grieving members of the public at Kensington Palace and down the Royal Mall. There was also a heated debate over whether the Queen should lower the flag at Buckingham Palace in tribute to Diana's death because, at that point, she was no longer 'a royal'. Finally, however, the Queen returned to London from Balmoral and accepted Charles's advice to lower the flag. A week after Diana's death the Queen made an unprecedented broadcast to the nation 'as the Queen and a grandmother.' The immediate crisis was over. But royal reputation was at a low ebb and the bereaved young princes were left with a mistrust of the media that they believed had killed their mother.

The objective

To deal with the mounting crisis of trust from the British public and secure the future of the British Monarchy in the long term.

The strategy

The royal family gradually phased out its age-old communications approach of keeping their heads down – best summed up in the motto: 'never complain, never explain and stick to public duties' – and instead implemented a new strategy that involved maintaining tradition (revolving around the Queen and viewing monarchy as a values system) while slowly adapting to the modern age (building a new team and more open attitude). In his 2015 book *Winners*, Alastair Campbell, who worked closely with the royal team during this period, identifies the key strategic words in this campaign as: Identity, Continuity, Recognition of Achievement and Service. Advisers, however, say there was never a strategy document or mission statement as such.

How the narrative unfolded ...

Phase 1 *1997 to 2002*

Michael Peat was treasurer to the Queen. The Prince of Wales's private secretary (head of Clarence House) was Sir Stephen Lamport, Mark Bolland was deputy private secretary, and Sandy Henney was official press secretary at Clarence House.

With the immediate crisis over following Diana's funeral, the process of modernization began to accelerate.

The Queen, looking ahead to her 2002 Golden Jubilee, was aware she needed to make changes to win back the affection that the royal family had clearly lost. She was aware that it was the next generation that was causing most of the negative headlines – and yet it was they who were the future. She needed to help rescue the standing of her children, especially Prince Charles.

Charles, who resided in his own household, also had his own plans to improve his personal image. To this end the head of Clarence House, Stephen Lamport, had brought in a specialist spin doctor, Mark Bolland. The team set about repositioning Charles as a single parent and caring father to the two young princes. This began with a 1997 visit to South Africa with Harry, and a ski trip to Canada. During both trips Bolland encouraged Charles to start acknowledging and engaging with the journalists. One of those journalists says: 'Charles came and chatted to all of us. There was clearly an emphasis on a more relaxed, fun-loving character. I think it was highly successful.'

The next stage was to make Charles's companion Camilla Parker Bowles, vilified by Diana and her team, more presentable to the public: a project known internally as 'operation PB'. Some aspects of this project were to backfire, such as an exclusive story agreed with *The Sun* newspaper about the first time Camilla met up with William. There was also an 'unofficial' and highly sympathetic biography of Charles that appeared on the anniversary of Diana's death, which appeared to be an unsubtle attempt at rewriting history. These initiatives managed to alienate other media and some within the royal household. More successful, however, was Bolland's masterminding of Charles and Camilla's first public outing together at a party at the Ritz Hotel, about which most British media had been tipped off. The event, at which the two were photographed holding hands and publicly leaving together for the first time, generated glowingly positive front pages for the tabloid press. The *Daily Mail* headline the following morning was one word: 'Together'.

Prince Charles and Camilla Parker Bowles on their first public outing as a couple
Source © Max Cisotti

At this point the emphasis of the media campaign switched to the two young princes. This was a tricky balance because of the need to position the boys as normal, responsible young men without jeopardizing the agreement between the royal family and the media that the young royals' privacy should be respected. And this time it was Charles's official press secretary Sandy Henney who messed up, by offering first access to images of Prince William at Eton College to the *Daily Telegraph* – much to the anger of other newspapers. Branded 'sneaky Sandy' in one rival paper, Henney resigned.

Mark Bolland continued to spin on behalf of Charles. A major success was getting Charles, Camilla and William to attend the 10th birthday party of the Press Complaints Commission, which further improved the royals' relations with the still sore media.

Eventually, however, Bolland went too far. His briefing against Prince Edward during a row over footage of William's arrival at St Andrew's University, and his attempt to spin a newspaper story 'Harry's Drugs Shame' in 2002 about Prince Harry being caught smoking cannabis, in Charles's favour, are said to have prompted the Queen to put her foot down, leading to Bolland's dismissal.

In retrospect, Bolland, although he had a tendency to play people off against one another, may have provided exactly what was required in this period. He rebuilt bridges with the media and repositioned Camilla for a future role.

Phase 2 *2003 to 2011*

Head of Clarence House was now Michael Peat; Paddy Harverson was hired as the first director of communications.

In 2002 Sir Michael Peat had become the Prince of Wales's principal private secretary and set a goal for a 'proper reassessment' of Charles by his 60th birthday in 2008.

According to Richard Kay, at that time the *Daily Mail*'s royal correspondent, Peat believed Charles's existing press operation to be 'leaking like a colander' and insisted on a more tightly-run ship. There was certainly a greater emphasis on duty and professionalism. There may even have been a recognition among the key members of the team that neither the Queen nor Charles was likely to change fundamentally as people, so the key was to find new ways of presenting them.

Key to this was the hire, in 2004, of Paddy Harverson as the first director of communications at Clarence House. The team agreed that there should be a major strategy shift, particularly towards broadcast media. In the early days Harverson took no nonsense from the tabloids, insisting on corrections and a right to reply to any negative articles that appeared. When he arrived, the Prince of Wales and the press were pretty much at war. Relations were particularly poor with the *Daily Mail* and the *Daily Express*. Meanwhile, *The Sun* and the *Daily Mirror* were trying to create mayhem, their editors possessing little respect for the royals.

Harverson, who prefers not to give interviews on his work for the royals, does admit that there followed a 'very clear attempt to move the focus from the personal to the professional.'

With the 'Camilla question' resolved, media interest had shifted to the two young princes, whose education was drawing to a close. William, schooled at the University of St Andrews, was mature enough to handle the media. The less academic Harry, on the other hand, left formal education at 18, meaning there was a two-year gap before he was due to join the army. This left him largely unprotected from the media. The younger prince was also prone to more hedonistic behaviour. As one royal correspondent at the time puts it: 'The media narrative became "sensible Wills and wild-child Harry"; this meant the latter's wild behaviour was somewhat exaggerated.'

'We decided to focus on broadcast documentaries,' explains Harverson. 'And we wanted to treat broadcasters differently, much more enthusiastically than before. Now broadcasters were invited to discuss specific ideas with us.'

As part of this approach Harverson agreed an exclusive ITN documentary about Prince Harry's volunteering trip to Lesotho. It was to prove a watershed moment for his media image. The young prince took his own photos, which were made available to the world's media. As a result Harry was able to display a dedicated compassionate nature with the African children, which reminded many of his mother, Diana.

Prince Harry volunteering in Maseru, Lesotho, 2013
Source PA Images

In 2004 *The Guardian* wrote:

> The royal household is not the suspicious, resentful place of yore.
> This is now, as Sir Michael Peat, the prince's private secretary, reminded
> correspondents at the reception on Wednesday evening, a beacon of
> openness and approachability, where they have briefings and speak
> on the record and where the phrase 'no comment' rarely passes their
> lips. This is a court which no longer briefs anonymously against
> other princelings who are thought to be getting too uppity and where
> Charles's old crowd – his former spin doctor Mark Bolland and his
> ex-equerry Michael Fawcett – have been quietly moved away.

But it was still far from plain sailing for Harverson and his team,
particularly with the Rupert Murdoch-owned tabloids, with whom
the press operation fought a running battle. In 2005, just two weeks
before Holocaust Memorial Day, the 20-year-old Prince Harry turned
up at a 'colonials and natives' costume party dressed as a Nazi. *The
Sun* published a photo of the prince wearing a swastika armband and
a Rommel-like desert uniform. In a statement the prince told the public:
'I'm very sorry if I have caused any offence. It was a poor choice of
costume, and I apologize.'

In the spring/summer of 2005 William graduated and Charles and Camilla got married, with the ceremony orchestrated by Harverson. Generally the broadcasters were playing ball and focusing on the professional duties of the royals. The media approach extended globally with a glowing profile of Prince Charles on CBS's *60 Minutes* in September 2005.

And yet the tabloid press continued to pick up highly personal stories. It was at this time that Clarence House began to suspect that some papers were hacking into private voicemails. It alerted the police. This was the beginning of the phone-hacking scandal that would shake the world and, ironically, ultimately help shift power from the media to the royals (see phone-hacking scandal, p 71).

The year 2007 was to prove a landmark in the public reinvention of the royal family. In January it emerged that William was about to become engaged to Kate Middleton, whom he had been dating since his time at the University of St Andrews. Middleton, as a commoner, did not at that time enjoy the protection of the royal media machine. In a number of unsavoury incidents she was hounded by the British media, reminding many of Diana's treatment. As a result Harverson and his team managed to get a new agreement on privacy from the media, which was more sympathetic.

August 2007 marked the 10th anniversary of Diana's death and Clarence House's strategy was to be proactive with the media and to consciously 'own' this event. Harverson says: 'When the tenth anniversary of Diana's death was looming, we got on with our own plans. Six months ahead we announced a concert and a memorial service, so before the media had even started to think about it we were out there and the princes were effectively saying: "this is our mother, our memories, discount everything else." We were on the front foot, less reactive than in the past.'

Nevertheless battles continue to be fought, not least with the BBC. The state broadcaster was forced to apologize in 2007 over a misleading trailer for a documentary called *A Year with the Queen* when it appeared to show Her Majesty storming out of a photoshoot.

By 2008 media coverage was almost exclusively focused on William and Harry's military careers. And in November of that year Peat and Harverson's 're-evaluation of Charles' project was complete, with a BBC1 documentary *The Passionate Prince* to mark the Prince of Wales's 60th birthday. At the time Nick Vaughan-Barratt, executive producer, said:

> This important documentary sheds new light on the Prince of Wales. Many people have a view about the prince but few people know him well; this film looks behind and beyond the headlines at the man himself. It shows the prince using his substantial influence to further a wide variety of causes – some of them unfashionable, some controversial – and it provides a rare opportunity to hear him speaking directly, not just about what he does but why he is so passionate about the many causes he espouses.

On 29 April 2011, nearly 14 years since Diana's death, the wedding of Prince William, Duke of Cambridge, and Kate Middleton took place. The event was considered a spectacular blending of tradition and modernity. In the UK the TV audience was 24 million and the event was screened live in 180 countries with an audience of more than 300 million people worldwide. The media operation was orchestrated by Harverson, who quit Clarence House in November

Wedding of the Duke and Duchess of Cambridge,
29 April 2011
Source Getty Images: Sean Gallup/Staff

that year to set up his own PR agency. But also crucial was Miguel Head, who by then was William and Harry's press secretary. He went on to become private secretary to the Duke of Cambridge.

Significantly, the event was also a culmination of Clarence House's hard-gained new media experience. At the time, the wedding was the biggest-ever live event on the internet. Harverson and his team had worked with Google for months to avoid the 'PrinceOfWales' website crashing on the day, and to screen the action via YouTube and other social media.

Following all of this, by late 2011, the percentage of people who thought the country would be worse off without the Crown had grown by 15 points on 1997, to 63 per cent.

Postscript ...

In August 2012, the Queen featured in a famously funny sketch during the opening ceremony of the London Olympics, where she was filmed talking to Daniel Craig's incarnation of James Bond. In the dark days of 1997 one couldn't imagine such a media stunt. 2012 was also the year of Queen Elizabeth II's Diamond Jubilee, and according to pollsters Ipsos MORI by now she enjoyed an approval rate in the United Kingdom of 90 per cent. Ipsos MORI's director of political analysis, Professor Roger Mortimore, said: 'This has been a triumphant jubilee year. After a rocky period in the 1990s, public support for the Monarchy and the Queen now looks as strong as it has been for many years. Most of the public now expect the Monarchy to survive well into the future, and that is probably the best guarantee that it will do so.' According to a YouGov poll in January 2014, the Queen was the most admired person in the United Kingdom with almost 20 per cent of the vote. Internationally she was the 17th most admired woman in the world.

This is not to say that there are not still problems with the media strategy. In August 2012 Harry was pictured at a 'strip billiards party' in Las Vegas. The action was caught on mobile phones with British media at first refusing to use the pictures on privacy grounds. Eventually *The Sun* decided to run the pictures on the basis that they were 'everywhere on the internet anyway'. And in September 2012 foreign paparazzi photographed Kate Middleton topless in France, encouraging the royal lawyers to go into overdrive. Despite years of building bridges with the media, incidents such as this, particularly involving foreign journalists, create familiar tensions between the royals and the media.

Nevertheless, the modern charm offensive continues on a global scale. Prince Harry's heavy involvement in the Paralympic-style sporting event, The Invictus Games, in March 2014, raised his popularity even further.

ON REFLECTION

- This campaign is characterized by a number of strong executives – from the Queen to Sir Michael Peat – as well as a new generation of astute media operators exemplified by Mark Bolland and Paddy Harverson. This evolving 'team' helped modernize and professionalize the British Monarchy. There is a sense of leadership from 1997 onwards, and even more so from 2003, which was vital to this campaign's success.

- The campaign demonstrates how an institution can harness its own visual content, including the redesign of the **www.princeofwales.gov.uk** website prior to the 2011 royal wedding based on previous user metrics and an insight into the power and reach of social media.

- As well as the effective use of negotiated documentaries, the team also understood the power of the single, exclusive photograph, such as the still of Prince Harry's 20th birthday, which showed Charles and his two sons relaxed and having fun.

- It proved that in this age of 24-7 media and intense scrutiny of anyone in public life, even an ancient and venerable institution can productively employ modern media management techniques.

- However, some would argue there is now so much compliance from the British media that there is no real relationship, let alone trust, between the royals and the fourth estate. William is still thought to fundamentally dislike the media, while his father Charles could be gearing up for another difficult period. The media have investigated the pressure that Charles had applied to politicians over the past decade by writing personal letters displaying his strong opinions on certain issues – a story known as 'the spider memos' because of the Prince's spidery handwriting.

- In conclusion, this was an uneven and often robust battle but stands as one of the greatest reputational turnarounds in modern history.

Britain's phone-hacking scandal

The phone-hacking scandal was a controversy that flared up in 2005 but stayed high on the public agenda for the next decade. It principally involved the now defunct Sunday tabloid, *News of the World* and other British newspapers owned by Rupert Murdoch's News International group. Journalists were found to have hacked into the personal voicemails of celebrities, politicians and members of the royal family in the pursuit of news stories.

Following a suspicious story in the *News of the World* in November 2005, which could only have been obtained from a voicemail message, the Metropolitan Police investigated and found that royal editor Clive Goodman and private investigator Glenn Mulcaire had remotely accessed the voicemail accounts belonging to Prince William's aides. The court heard that Mulcaire had also hacked into the messages of supermodel Elle Macpherson, publicist Max Clifford and football agent Sky Andrew. Goodman and Mulcaire were sentenced to four- and six-months' imprisonment respectively. On the same day, Andy Coulson resigned as editor of the *News of the World*, while insisting that he had no knowledge of any illegal activities. He was later to become Prime Minister David Cameron's director of communications.

The story smouldered for another five years before catching light when it was revealed in July 2011 that the phones of murdered schoolgirl Milly Dowler and relatives of deceased British soldiers and victims of the 7 July 2005 London bombings had also

▶

been hacked. The resulting public outcry against News Corporation led to several high-profile resignations, including that of Dow Jones CEO Les Hinton and News International CEO Rebekah Brooks. A week later Murdoch announced he was closing the 168-year-old *News of the World*. British Prime Minister David Cameron announced that a public inquiry, known as the Leveson Inquiry, would look into phone-hacking and consider the wider culture and ethics of the British newspaper industry. Coulson and Brooks were arrested. The former later went to prison, the latter was acquitted.

The Leveson report, published in November 2012, found that the existing Press Complaints Commission was not fit for purpose, and recommended a new independent body, which would have a range of sanctions available to it. Leveson rejected the characterization of his proposal as 'statutory regulation of the press'.

Despite being publicly censured, Murdoch continues to be a powerful media operator in the UK and internationally. His British newspaper operation has been rebranded as News UK and continues to run *The Sun*, *The Times* and *The Sunday Times*, albeit with much stricter rules of journalistic conduct. A new voluntary press regulator called IPSO was set up in September 2014. And, generally, tabloid newspapers are perceived to be better behaved since Leveson, arguably increasing the relative PR power of institutions such as the royal family.

The Leveson Inquiry also called into question what was seen by many as an unhealthy closeness between some politicians, journalists and PR professionals, which has made all parties a little more cautious since.

Acknowledgement

Winners: And how they succeed (2015) Alastair Campbell, published by Hutchinson, Random House

Part Two
New approaches in global entertainment and sport, based on coalition and creativity

Chapter Four
Start Me Up
Reinventing
the Rolling Stones –
1981–1982

Introduction

In 1981 the Rolling Stones embarked on a rock 'n' roll experiment – an ambitious live tour of major stadiums in both North America and Europe, and a fresh approach to communicating rock music. The Stones were to prove the naysayers wrong on all counts. The new strategy rejuvenated the band's reputation; generated a record amount of revenue for a live tour; and set new commercial ambitions for music bands around the world.

Why the campaign shook the world

This campaign literally shook the world. Well, at least it shook those parts where the Rolling Stones' distinctive blues–rock boomed out. More importantly, the campaign shook up the music and entertainment business at the time, encouraging other acts to embrace the concept of 'the stadiums tour'. The Stones were the first band to embark on such tours, opening up exciting new international markets for major rock acts.

Alan Edwards hosting 'Always Print the Myth' exhibition at the Victoria and Albert Museum, London, 2015
Source Julian Dodd

The campaign also successfully rejuvenated one of the greatest rock 'n' roll bands the world has seen. It helped rescue their reputation and motivate fans after a decidedly inglorious period during the mid-1970s. After 1982, the band was seen less as ageing, decadent corruptors of youth, and more as a national institution.

The 1981 US tour alone generated more than $50 million in revenue, twice what any previous tour had achieved, and there were innovative spin-off products. In short, the frontman and business manager, Mick Jagger, had turned what began as a 1960s counter-cultural phenomenon into a thriving modern business.

After 1981's *Tattoo You* album (on which *Start Me Up* was the opening song) the Rolling Stones may never again record a truly great rock LP, but the accompanying tour finally established the band as a global brand. The Stones had created enough buzz to be perceived as one of the world's must-see live acts for future generations: a phenomenon that endures right up to the present day.

Why is the campaign great?

From the early days the Rolling Stones, and particularly Mick Jagger, were acutely aware of their image and the power of smart communication. In the 1960s the Stones' early manager, Andrew Loog Oldham, worked with the band to position them as the 'bad boys' to the Beatles' lovable and clean-cut image. The Stones deliberately spurned suits and grew their hair longer. Oldham was responsible for widely reprinted tabloid headlines such as 'Would you let your daughter marry a Rolling Stone?' Of course the inevitable reaction from rebellious daughters at the time would be 'Yes please!'

Nearly two decades on, we saw a new approach from the Stones towards communications and marketing. Jagger made media relations a top priority, with advance press tours that displayed the same ambition and focus as the live performances. The wider communications campaign was unusually professional and sophisticated for the period, with a notably vibrant-yet-controlled approach for a group of musicians who were now in their late thirties.

Jagger and his band also embraced new types of visual branding, sponsorship and affiliate marketing, opening the eyes of entertainment marketers everywhere.

The cast

Sir Mick Jagger (born 1943) – knighted in 2003

Make no mistake, this was Mick Jagger's campaign. After the band's acrimonious split with their second manager, Allen Klein, in 1971, Jagger took control of business affairs and managed the group from that point onwards, in collaboration with his friend and colleague Prince Rupert Loewenstein. (Loewenstein was the Stones' financial manager until retiring in 2007. He died in 2014.)

Michael Philip Jagger was born into a middle-class family in Kent, England in July 1943. Even while sharing a flat in London with Keith Richards and Brian Jones in his early twenties Jagger continued with his business course at the London School of Economics. He had seriously considered becoming either a journalist or a politician. Knighted in 2003 for services to music, Jagger has always networked well and worked hard.

Jagger gradually became aware of the power of the media in the Stones' fortunes – something he talked about openly at their 50th anniversary event in London in 2012. He was grateful for the work that early manager Andrew Loog Oldman had done in the 1960s, positioning them as the rebellious bad boys to the more respectable Beatles. By the late 1970s he was taking more control of the band's comms and commercial strategy. Alan Edwards, the Stones' PR adviser at that time, said Jagger 'had clearly grown up understanding and appreciating the media, and with a vision for communications and marketing'. Edwards describes Jagger by the 1980s thus: 'He was the businessman at the head of a corporation – he just happened to have long hair.'

Bill Graham
Source Photo by Mark Sarfati

Bill Graham (1931–1991), concert promoter

Bill Graham was a US impresario and rock concert promoter from the 1960s until his death in 1991 in a helicopter crash. In 1981 his firm, Raindrop Productions, promoted and directed the Rolling Stones tour of that year. Graham provided the sound, lighting and infrastructure for the shows. He even announced the band's arrival on stage each night in his trademark booming voice.

During World War Two Graham had fled from Germany, and then France to escape the Holocaust in Europe. He eventually settled in a foster home in New York before going to high school in the city and graduating with a business degree. The charismatic entrepreneur later bought a live venue in California and became a legendary figure in the American rock 'n' roll scene of the 1970s. Following his death in 1991 his company, Bill Graham Presents (BGP), was taken over by a group of employees. Graham's sons remained a core part of the new management team. Through many years, and many different owners, the business eventually morphed into Live Nation – now the world's largest concert production/promotion company.

★ THE CAMPAIGN'S (RISING) STAR ★
Alan Edwards

Alan Edwards is one of the outstanding celebrity PRs of his generation, but when he started handling media for the Rolling Stones he was just 25.

Obsessed with newspapers and magazines from an early age, Edwards had landed his first job in PR at the age of 16, working for the legendary 1960s/70s rock PR Keith Altham, who handled The Who and Marc Bolan at the time. Edwards quickly made a name for himself representing the young punk and new wave bands that were emerging, including The Damned and Blondie. His passion for media prompted him to create on-the-road fanzines for the bands he represented in order to create buzz and foster loyal followings.

In 1981 Edwards had recently broken away to set up his own consultancy, Modern Publicity. British music promoter Harvey Goldsmith recommended him to the Rolling Stones who were embarking on a world tour. Edwards subsequently spent months on the road with Jagger and co, handling international media, and ended up working for them for nine years. 'I probably learned more about PR and marketing from Mick Jagger than anyone,' says Edwards. 'He was great with the media, and obsessed with reputation, brand and commercial development. Mick taught me about interview technique, prep and analysis. He also taught me about the need for physical fitness and self-discipline. Ever since working for Mick I've gone for a run every single day.'

In the early 1990s Edwards worked for such talent as Janet Jackson and Prince. And in 1995 he set up the reputation management consultancy that he still runs today, Outside Organisation. Outside meant external, independent PR advice and also happened to be the name of a David Bowie concept album released that year. Bowie was another client and 'artist' who had a huge influence on Edwards. 'David was a campaign in his own right; he was in a whole other space. He is a genius,' Edwards says.

Indeed there are few major rock acts that Edwards hasn't represented at some point since, which was one of the reasons that Virgin Records' boss Paul Conroy was keen to put him on the Spice Girls project in 1997 when the band was becoming huge but seemingly spinning out of control. 'Paul told the team that I was ideal because I understood brands on a global level,' remembers Edwards. As he became a trusted adviser to Victoria Adams, she later recommended his abilities to David Beckham (see Chapter 5).

Despite a stream of celebrity clients (he has since looked after Naomi Campbell and Amy Winehouse) and his relentless lifestyle, Edwards retains a uniquely unassuming, relaxed and engaging demeanour. He has the sort of accent and style associated with London in the 'swinging sixties' and this class-transcending cool wins over stars and media alike. Edwards puts strong relationships at the heart of his media strategies. The snappily dressed PR is very much part of the London scene. He is friendly with most of the UK's tabloid and magazine editors, and spends many an evening or weekend accompanying them to major gigs or football matches. These personal relationships with journalists enable him to construct mutually beneficial narratives for his clients.

Many of Outside's former employees have gone on to great things, such as Stuart Bell who took Paul McCartney with him as a client, but Edwards remains the adviser to turn to for many celebrities who run into a crisis. As such he has built strong links with entertainment lawyers. And when it comes to positioning celebrities as truly long-term brands, few in the UK have Edwards' depth and breadth of experience.

THE CAMPAIGN

The context

In the late 1970s rock music was undergoing a revolution. The big acts of the early 1970s such as The Who, Genesis and the Rolling Stones, were increasingly portrayed by the music and style media as 'dinosaurs'. The record-buying public was becoming tired of what they saw as increasingly overindulgent concept albums featuring overblown guitar and drum solos. A new generation of energetic, aggressive punk and new wave groups, from The Ramones in New York to the Sex Pistols in London, felt exciting and portrayed a fresh, young image for rock 'n' roll.

For the Stones in particular this was proving a difficult period. The line-up had become unsettled with guitarist Mick Taylor leaving the band and, after a number of experimental replacements, Ronnie Wood joining. There were many reported drug-related problems, including addiction and the arrest of band members for possession of illegal substances in the UK and abroad. For many, particularly in America, the Rolling Stones were viewed as a corrupting force for the young, which ultimately restricted their commercial appeal.

Music critics had also grown increasingly dismissive of the group's output following the great *Exile on Main Street* album of 1972. Subsequent record sales failed to meet expectations. Many writers criticized the band, which had originally formed back in 1962, for living and looking like decadent, ageing millionaires. Their music was by now often dismissed as stagnant or irrelevant.

The objective

To reinvent the band as relevant to a new generation and to a wider global audience. Success would be measured in the quantity and diversity of people paying to see the Stones live; in the number of album sales; and in the sustainable revenues that the band could generate.

The strategy

To use the tour and the accompanying communications to appear fresh, youthful, healthy and professional. To take a whole new approach to marketing: making media communications a priority and treating touring like a political campaign; embracing new types of commercial tie-up; tightly controlling the use of Stones' imagery and content; and expanding this content into new media channels.

How the narrative unfolded ...

The now accomplished music PR Alan Edwards admits that before being hired to handle media for the Rolling Stones in 1981, he was also one of their young and disillusioned acolytes: 'I had been a huge Stones fan and had gone to see them play Earls Court in 1976. But like many others I was disappointed. They were sloppy and lacklustre on stage. Indeed this gig was credited for prompting many musicians in the punk–rock movement to set up their own bands. As someone who worked in communications I realized the whole thing needed getting hold of.' Five years later, still only 25, Edwards was to join up with the band and be a part of the tour that helped revive their reputation.

Phase 1 *The US tour – 1981*

By 1981 the band's musical influence was increasing again. The recent albums *Some Girls* and *Emotional Rescue* had been well received, and the budding *Tattoo You* (released 24 August 1981) was creating a positive buzz, which built pressure, particularly from the music media, to undertake another international tour. Although guitarists Keith Richards and Ronnie Wood were keen, Jagger is said to have been reluctant after the exhausting previous US tour in 1978, which had featured 25 venues of variable size and quality and enjoyed limited commercial success.

Jagger eventually relented, on the understanding that this time he would control every detail of the tour. First up was a 25-stop US tour, which would include consistently huge venues such as Madison

Square Garden in New York and the 95,000-capacity JFK Stadium in Philadelphia. Even the bombastic US promoter Bill Graham reported directly to Mick, who commissioned Japanese designer Kazuhide Yamazaki to design the stage set and posters. Jagger was quoted in the book *According to the Rolling Stones*, by Dora Loewenstein and Philip Dodd, as saying: 'Most concerts that took place outdoors at the time were played during the day, probably because it was cheaper, I don't know. So we had the bright, bright primary colours ... and we had these enormous images of a guitar, a car and a record – an Americana idea – which worked very well for afternoon shows.'

Jagger was also determined to oversee directly a more professional media operation. By the time Edwards was recommended to Jagger by British promoter Harvey Goldsmith in 1981 the US tour was already in full swing. 'I was called to a meeting with Mick in New York,' Edwards recalls. 'The interview lasted about an hour. He quizzed me on the circulation figures for the UK press and asked who owned the various newspapers. He asked me all about the European media, which fortunately I had got to know from my days looking after punk bands, albeit from the back of a van. He knew that he wanted truly international PR.' Edwards must have impressed because he was immediately hired to manage the media operation for the European tour in the spring.

'I later realized that my hiring was a piece of shrewd marketing itself,' reflects Edwards. 'I think Mick liked the idea of this punky kid running around with the band, wearing football shirts. It was all about the band looking younger and having a reinvigorated image. He had realized that every decade bands have to recharge themselves for the next generation.'

The US tour proved an early financial triumph – the largest grossing tour of not only 1981, but for several years to come. Three million Americans attended the concerts, grossing $50 million in ticket sales. In late 1981 The *New York Times* wrote: 'The tour is expected to be the most profitable in the history of rock 'n' roll; its sheer size has been staggering ... ticket requests for these shows ran into the millions ...'.

Jagger was also encouraged by the positive impact the tour had made on the band's reputation in America. The *New York Times*:

'Suddenly, everyone wants to see the Rolling Stones – their older fans are in their 30s and 40s, like the Stones themselves; their youngest fans are barely into their teens. "The crowds were young, real young in Florida," Mick Jagger noted with evident relish as a make-up man applied pancake make-up to his face, a few minutes before the group was scheduled to go onstage in Atlanta.'

And following the US leg, in January 1982 US rock magazine *Rolling Stone* wrote: 'The Rolling Stones' 1981 US tour was more than just an artistic triumph. It was also a spectacular financial coup – the headiest windfall in rock 'n' roll history. In its aftermath, Mick Jagger stands revealed as a master career strategist of the first order – the toughest, shrewdest businessman to emerge on the entertainment scene since Bob Hope and Frank Sinatra.'

Phase 2 *The European tour – 1982*

The next step was to replicate and further develop the formula for Europe. The band hadn't toured Europe for six years. Jagger and Bill Graham planned a 32-date tour of continental stadiums from May 1982 to the end of July, including the Estadio Vincente Calderón in Madrid and the Olympiastadion in Munich. The Rolling Stones even managed to release a live album *Still Life (American Concert 1981)* in time for the European leg.

Edwards describes the unusual UK media launch for the European tour, in London: 'It was carefully staged in a very cool underground dance club of the time, called Le Beat Route in Soho. All the characters from the Fleet Street press were there, such as the legendary *Daily Express* reporter Judith Simons, who was known affectionately as "Fag Ash Lil" because she always had a cigarette hanging out of her mouth. I was surprised because Mick introduced me to the media rather than the other way round. The story appeared on the front page of *The Sun* next day, with the 38-year-old Mick looking young and happy, and a caption saying "We are going to rock Europe".'

Jagger once again controlled the entire marketing mix. The famous 'lips and tongue' logo – originally created by John Pasche for the 1971

Sticky Fingers album – featured prominently on all posters and promotional material. 'Mick ensured the use of the logo was tightly controlled,' recalls Edwards. And the band broke new commercial ground by signing up tour sponsors, including cassette tape manufacturer TDK. Jagger sold exclusive advertising rights on all tour tickets to fragrance firm Jōvan Musk for $1 million, attracting considerable attention in the business media at the time; this mainstream fragrance looked at odd with the Stones' 'bad boys' image. The band behaved well on tour however, and rock tour corporate sponsorships soon became the norm. Jōvan Musk was also given a large block of tickets for each gig, which were given away via radio phone-ins. David Miller, Jōvan's advertising director at the time, was quoted as saying that they signed the deal because they were convinced the Stones' audience now included two distinct generations, ranging from the mid-teens to the mid-thirties.

Before the gigs even began Jagger and Edwards embarked on a two-day, ten-city media tour of Europe involving a press conference in each. Edwards describes it as 'a presidential-style media campaign': 'We would fly into Munich in the morning, Düsseldorf at lunchtime, Paris in the afternoon. For each city Mick had asked me to brief him on the hot local rock acts, the local football team, the local politicians. We worked out all the angles in advance and practised them. He wanted dossiers on journalists in advance; what their interests were and so on. It meant he would be entering a different sort of dialogue with them. But we always ensured we delivered the key messages about how to get tickets for the gig and the new album that was out. I even had to visit the local record stores in advance to make sure it was on sale there. It was an exhausting but incredibly thrilling thing to do. The support acts tended to be up-and-coming local groups and the band seemed really energized by the whole thing. They had booked all the European stadiums, which no one had done before. They understood, particularly Mick, that they had the potential to be a global brand.'

Edwards recalls that the tour was run by a tight management team with Bill Graham working in conjunction with the local promoters – Harvey Goldsmith in the UK – and executives from the Stones' record label, but that he worked directly for Jagger and the band.

'They saw me as "the kid". I was very involved in who was attending from the media. Mick was heavily focused on the media coverage on a daily basis. The whole band exploited media photo opportunities. And it definitely wasn't an exercise in sycophancy – it was an exercise in marketing. Mick would specifically ask me why we hadn't got more radio in Marseilles, why not the *El País* paper in Spain, what messages were not coming across well enough.

'The band members were very keen that their efforts in one territory were exploited in another. For example, if they did an interview or photo-call in Italy, they wanted to make sure it was used in the UK or Scandinavia etc. Really it was the same as any modern global brand: keep the images and messages rolling out territory by territory.'

Edwards says that after each gig, while the Stones went off to dinner, he would hang out with the local journalists and get a sense of how they felt about the tour. 'It looked like a glamorous lifestyle but I never got to eat in the best restaurants or go to the parties' he sighs. 'The band members wanted a media report under their door every morning, including the reviews of the previous night, and a schedule of media they would be doing the next day. Of course there were no mobile phones or laptops in those days. I had to run off to the local railway station to get the early editions of papers, then I sat on a hotel typewriter to translate the foreign coverage. And all this was before the day had really started.'

One key message for the media was that, with the death of John Lennon and the split of Led Zeppelin (both December 1980), the Stones were now the last big 60s acts still going, so fans would be advised to see them play live now. Indeed one UK paper's review of a 1982 British gig used the headline: 'This could be the last time!'

Another message, says Edwards, was Jagger's now seemingly healthy and wholesome lifestyle. 'Mick understood the power of media pictures. We knew that if he went out jogging there was bound to be a tabloid photographer waiting in the bushes somewhere, so we were prepared for that. I used to jog along 20 yards behind him. At that time it was likely to be [famed celebrity photographer] Richard Young.' Again the approach paid off: pictures appeared in the press on both sides of the Atlantic (including *Life* magazine) of Jagger out jogging with a professional look on his tanned visage.

The band's professionalism and Edwards' hard work reaped major reputational benefits as the tour was well received in both foreign media and back home. In 1982 *Rolling Stone* wrote: 'It is a tribute to Jagger's genius for manipulation that the media so eagerly embraced the band's new, non-threatening image.' To pun on a famous Stones track, the band was beginning to prove that, with the right strategy, you can always get what you want.

Overall it was reported that the Stones were making $1 million per night after tour expenses, helped by the fact that there were so many spin-off products. In 1983 they released a live concert film called *Let's Spend the Night Together* documenting the tour. In New Zealand and Australia it had the alternative title *Time is on our Side* and was called *Rocks Off* in Germany.

By the end of the year the band had signed a new four-album recording deal with a new label, CBS Records, for a reported $50 million – then the biggest record deal in history.

Postscript ...

This was actually the last time the Rolling Stones toured America and Europe until 1989, which saw the massive Steel Wheels/Urban Jungle Tour. One of the reasons for the delay was the growing division between Jagger and Keith Richards, which the latter famously described as 'World War Three'.

Edwards looked after the media for the Stones until 1990 and admits it was 'challenging' with relations between the two main characters so strained and each briefing against each other in the media: 'It was like an early version of Tony Blair and Gordon Brown'. However, the formula was set for continuing stadium tours and the successful Steel Wheels/Urban Jungle tour is reported to have grossed $98 million from the box office alone, and up to another $60 million from Budweiser's sponsorship.

From 1990 onwards, Bernard Doherty handled the PR for the Rolling Stones, under the auspices of his newly-formed agency. Doherty was respected for handling the media for the Live Aid Concert in 1985. At the time of writing, Doherty's firm, LD Communications, continues

Rolling Stones perform at Glastonbury Festival, 29 June 2013
Source Getty Images: Dave J Hogan/Contributor

to look after the Stones. Doherty expertly steered the Stones through the next two-and-a-half decades, helping their global appeal endure.

The band continued to embark on major tours every few years. In 2012/13 the 50 & Counting Tour celebrated the 50th anniversary of the band. It saw the Stones headline Hyde Park and the Glastonbury Festival. On the morning of the Glastonbury gig, limited extracts of which were screened live on the BBC, the broadcaster's flagship radio news programme *Today* based itself at the site, with anchorman John Humphrys conducting a lengthy live interview with Mick Jagger.

ON REFLECTION

- The Rolling Stones' campaign exemplified how talented musicians and performers could embrace the best contemporary thinking on commercial development and marketing communications.

- The Stones were one of the first rock bands to sign deals with fragrance brands and car companies, embracing fresh techniques such as exclusive sponsorship of tickets and innovative promotions.

- Mike Jagger was prescient in his controlled exploitation of the band's content, such as merchandise, logos and the distribution of films of their live concerts. Crucially, the Stones were one of the first bands to realize that their albums could be a memento of a tour rather than the other way round. More than three decades before they became buzzwords the Stones were recognizing the power of 'content' and 'owned media', even pushing their boundaries.

- The band applied strict access conditions to the media, which enabled them to control messages effectively. By the time Jagger talked to journalists, he knew precisely the messages and images that he was trying to deliver, tailored to that particular outlet. The band monitored the coverage and adjusted their schedule if the PR programme was not delivering. The Stones, like all savvy media operators, understood the power of selective pictures, stunts and photo-calls.

- Like any campaign, it wasn't perfect. There were still damaging personal stories in the media afterwards. And like many an elite team, there were serious – almost terminal – spats between band members. Jagger may have established himself as an institution but the establishment itself still had a big problem with him. It is said that the Queen refused to present Jagger's knighthood herself (he was knighted by the Prince of Wales in December 2003) allegedly because of his decadent past. But this has its advantages too. We don't want our rock stars to become too acceptable, do we?

- The Stones' experiment of 1981/82 ensured large stadium tours became a mainstay of the entertainment industry hence. Few major rock acts now would consider anything else and on a regular basis (although there is still the occasional need to play smaller venues to restore grassroots credibility). Moreover with the crisis in recorded music revenues brought on by the advent of the internet, live tours have become increasingly important commercially for any music act.

Acknowledgement

According to the Rolling Stones (2003) edited by Dora Loewenstein and Philip Dodd, published by Weidenfeld and Nicolson

Chapter Five
A way beyond football
Brand David Beckham
– 1998–2013

Introduction

The campaign to transform David Beckham into one of the most recognized sports brands in the world has ripped up the rulebook when it comes to talent's relationship with business. Very few professional sportsmen or women go on to elevate their standing in the minds of the public following their retirement, let alone increase their financial status by continuing to develop the value of their brand.

The development of the David Beckham brand intersects with several other notable campaigns of this period, not least the pop career of the Spice Girls, the launch of the Victoria Beckham fashion label and the growth of Premier League football. It is necessary therefore to view Beckham's campaign to be perceived 'as more than just a football player' with these other campaigns, and the concurrent opportunities that emerged.

Why the campaign shook the world

In the summer of 1998 David Beckham, a promising 23-year-old English footballer ended his first World Cup in disgrace after being

Simon Fuller
Source XIX Entertainment

Beckham receives red card and is branded Britain's most hated man, World Cup finals, 1998
Source Getty Images: Bob Thomas/Contributor

sent off in a match versus Argentina that was to knock England out of the competition. Many appeared to blame Beckham for England's loss. He was later branded 'the most hated man in Britain' by the British media.

And yet by the time he finally retired from football in May 2013, Beckham was earning well over £30 million per year from commercial ventures and endorsements, from North America to China, and starting to embark on innovative new types of partnerships with fashion brands, hotel groups and media organizations.

By 2015 he was setting up his own Major League Soccer (MLS) football club in Miami and had launched a series of commercial partnerships. Brand experts are predicting he could soon oversee a $500 million business under his name. In 2015 an international YouGov poll of 25,000 people found Beckham to be the tenth 'most admired person in the world', just behind the Dalai Lama and Stephen Hawking.

Thanks to his own vision in 1998, his partnership with his wife Victoria, and the top advisers with which he surrounded himself, Beckham has transformed himself from controversial footballer into a recognized world ambassador for sport, fashion and fatherhood.

Why is the campaign great?

This long-term, international, personality-based campaign is notable for its ambition, clarity of purpose, innovation and brilliant perception management. David Beckham enjoys public awareness more akin to royalty or a large corporation, and as a result has also suffered the same challenges, slip-ups and crises along the way. The commercial partnerships strategy has been relentless and astute, the PR strong enough to build and protect his reputation over 15 eventful years.

Beckham displayed unusual bravery and determination via proactive communications and strategic planning to build his brand. From the very early days he recognized the power of his own image and content and his partners and advisers have managed these assets creatively and to their utmost global impact.

The cast

David Beckham (born 1975)

Beckham was one of the outstanding international footballers of his generation, winning 115 caps for his country (half of them as captain) and league championships in England, Spain, the USA and France. He was born to parents in the working-class area of Leytonstone, east London. He made his first team debut for Manchester United at the age of 17, alongside other British footballing legends such as Ryan Giggs and Paul Scholes. Unlike his much lauded peers, however, Beckham had the burning ambition to transcend football and become a global superstar and businessman; he loved fashion and wanted to explore pop culture. And he wasted no time and effort in achieving his aim.

Victoria Beckham, née Adams (born 1974)

By rights Victoria Beckham deserves her own campaign case study in transcending her original career as one of the Spice Girls to build a brand worth millions in the fashion world. Victoria has been a full and equal partner in developing the powerful brand 'The Beckhams'.

Victoria achieved fame in 1996 as a part of the Spice Girls, and was managed by Simon Fuller long before he'd become the Hollywood power player that he is today. It's said that Victoria was crucial to David's success in the early days of their marriage as someone who advised and supported him, despite being initially derided for her Essex accent and as someone 'clinging to David's talent', though she's since gone on to pursue her own business ambitions, setting up her eponymous fashion label worth $300 million. The Victoria Beckham label was named designer brand of the year in the UK in 2011 and 2014.

★ THE CAMPAIGN STAR ★
Simon Fuller

Born in 1960, and founder and owner of XIX Entertainment, British entrepreneur Simon Fuller has been described as a 'pop svengali', though this is misleading because his influence today extends beyond music, into fashion, retail, TV and sport, and he's probably better described as a global brand visionary, even a marketing genius. It was Simon Fuller who first introduced David to Victoria in the players' lounge after a Chelsea v Manchester United game in March 1997, but it wasn't until much later, under Fuller's management from 2003 onward, that they took the step to formally partner with him to develop their businesses as three-dimensional global brands.

The 'svengali' tag for Fuller, who is famously secretive and rarely does interviews, is a hangover from his early career in the music industry, which began in the early 1980s when he worked as a talent scout for Chrysalis Music. It was there that he discovered Paul Hardcastle, a DJ whose seminal dance track '19' became a No.1 hit, inspiring Fuller to branch out with his own management company '19 Entertainment'. In the mid-1990s he was the mastermind behind Girl Power and manager of the Spice Girls before creating a new ITV1 Saturday-night talent show called *Pop Idol* in 2001. *Pop Idol* was a game-changing moment for Fuller, as it later became *American Idol*, the most popular entertainment show of the last 10 years in America, making stars of Simon Cowell and Ryan Seacrest, Kelly Clarkson, Jordin Sparks and many others.

'Fuller had a natural ear for a hit song', remembers one colleague from that time. 'He used to love working with unknown artists, pitching them to the big labels and he loved the challenge of going up against the odds. But he never wanted to be in the spotlight. He wanted to move about unobserved'. This is a key insight and it's a remarkable story for an ordinary boy from Hastings in East Sussex. His friends describe him as being quietly spoken and modest, a lifelong Manchester United fan and someone who's keen to avoid the glare of publicity. But Fuller's strategic brain and talent for extracting the best from musicians and personalities was not lost on promoter Harvey Goldsmith: 'Fuller's genius is sensing what's possible in popular culture, and then developing that idea into a rip-roaring success. He's obviously incredibly persuasive but he seems like a very nice bloke. You don't see him hanging out with the stars at parties. His modus operandi is seeing opportunities, quietly grabbing them, staying under the radar, and delivering.'

In March 2005 Fuller sold his business 19 Entertainment to CKX in a cash-and-stock deal worth over $200 million and became a director of CKX which gave him creative control over all of CKX's assets, including the Elvis Presley Estate and the Muhammad Ali business, and, most importantly, real power in North America.

In 2010 he started XIX Entertainment with ambitions to create new ventures in partnership with talent. In addition to the Beckhams the new firm signed tennis player Andy Murray as he rose to win at Wimbledon and the F1 driver Lewis Hamilton, whom Fuller astutely moved from McLaren to a winning Mercedes team. Hamilton has since moved on but retains an enduring respect for his former manager, tweeting 'I love this guy' after being pictured alongside Fuller at the 2014 British Fashion Awards.

Fuller is not a classic PR man but Julian Henry, head of communications for XIX Entertainment London, explains, 'Simon is someone who believes in the power of great PR and who only wants the best for his partners. You can move mountains if you have a long-term view and if you're prepared to work hard towards a shared communication goal. When strategies are being discussed for any of our business ventures Fuller always wants to know what the optimum perception can be, and we build a plan as a team around what he wants to achieve.'

THE CAMPAIGN

The context

By the mid-1990s English football had come a long way since the dark days of the previous decade. English hooliganism led to 39 deaths at the European Cup Final at the Heysel Stadium in 1985 and English teams were banned from European competition for five years. In 1989 poor policing at the Hillsborough ground in Sheffield caused the tragic deaths of 96 Liverpool fans at an FA Cup semi-final. The subsequent Taylor Report set about cleaning up the game and introducing all-seater stadiums with proper facilities. In 1990 in Italy, England came within a penalty of reaching the World Cup final, creating the first modern English football stars: glamour was starting to return to football. And in 1992, with the backing of money from Rupert Murdoch's British Sky Broadcasting, the top tier of English football was rebranded as the Premier League with the aim of marketing the game to both brands and international audiences.

David Beckham had been a promising young player at Manchester United since 1991. But it was in 1996 that he grabbed media fame, scoring a stunning goal from the halfway line against Wimbledon FC. He was a key player in the United team that won the league title in 1997. But 1998 was to prove the pivotal year for Beckham. In January he became engaged to Victoria, better known as the Spice Girls star 'Posh Spice'. It was also a World Cup year and he was invited to join the England national squad in France. He made an instant impression in the third game, scoring against Columbia. However, in what was to be the final game, against Argentina, he was sent off for a petulant kick at Diego Simeone and England ended up losing the game. Much of the British media blamed Beckham for the defeat. Effigies were burned in the street and he was sent dog faeces in the post. By August 1998, Beckham was branded 'the most hated man in Britain' by the media.

The objective

David Beckham always believed in himself as an athlete but unlike most other sports stars he had ambitions stretching far beyond his footballing talent. His values as a player – hard work, determination, fair-play and the constant desire to overcome adversity – became the foundation for a career that only finally settled when he arrived in the United States, which was when he realized that he could be a global brand in his own right. The Beckham's family life in Los Angeles, his friendship with Tom Cruise, his visual referencing of movie stars like Steve McQueen, as well as the constant encouragement from his business partnership with Fuller finally gave David Beckham the self-belief to pursue his own American Dream.

The strategy

Initially Beckham's ambition was that of millions of other young sports stars. He simply wanted to play for Manchester United and England, although like many other Premier League footballers, he struggled initially to stand out from the crowd, appearing unable to present a defining image to TV viewers. This began to change as his fame increased and after he met Victoria who encouraged him to explore his creative instincts and masculinity in ways that challenged the way sports stars conventionally portrayed themselves.

But after leaving Manchester United in 2003, and with his wife Victoria and manager Simon Fuller at his side, his strategy became more focused and sophisticated: to create an iconic male figure that inspires and has broad appeal and recognition around the world, and which instils positive values in terms of respect, hard work and equality. Out of this would spring various potential businesses. Fuller explains: 'Our strategy was simply to make sure that everything we did with David commercially or with the media always had the same authenticity, integrity and scale to match David's position as the world's most iconic sportsman. Every small detail matters. It is better to do nothing than do the wrong thing.'

How the narrative unfolded ...

Phase 1 *1998 to 2003*

In his final years at Manchester United David Beckham was already pushing against the glass ceiling. When the respected music PR Alan Edwards and his agency Outside Organisation (see Chapter 4) first spent quality time with Beckham on 1 July 1998 it was at a Spice Girls concert at Madison Square Garden in New York. Edwards was handling PR for them and was introduced to Beckham by his fiancée, Victoria Adams.

'David was looking a bit lost when I met him,' recalls Edwards. 'He was shocked by the way the British media had turned on him after he was sent off in the final World Cup match.' Edwards, who was by then a highly experienced adviser to musicians, brought in all the recent British papers and sat down with David to talk calmly through the positives and negatives of the coverage.

Edwards helped plot Beckham's media 'restabilization' campaign, negotiating selective exposure in non-sports magazines such as *Esquire* and *Time Out*. 'These were not obvious places to see a footballer at the time,' Edwards points out.

Beckham's football PR was handled by his club, Manchester United, where Paddy Harverson (see Chapter 3) was communications director at the time. Instead, Edwards' job was to build Beckham's brand outside football; an ambition that burned deeply within the young star. 'I first realized this when I took a journalist up to interview David in December 1998,' recalls Edwards. 'We did the interview in a hotel by the station and David was still incredibly shy.' Having steered Beckham through the interview, Edwards was then invited back to Beckham's house for dinner. 'David was living in what used to be called "digs", in a terraced street in Salford. The first drama was we couldn't get the lights on until I found a coin for the meter. Then he couldn't find a can opener for the baked beans. Eventually we sat down and I asked him what he wanted a PR adviser to do. Usually the first question young stars asked me was "Can you get me a deal on a Ferrari" or "Can you get me into such and such club?" But, with

David, this mesmerizing vision suddenly poured out. He felt very strongly about women's sport; he hated racism and homophobia and wanted to help fight against it; he thought soccer in America had been underdeveloped. It was one of those moments when I realized I was in the presence of greatness.'

Beckham also had strong views on the development of his own brand, says Edwards: 'David suggested we do an Elvis mock-up for the *Sunday Times* style section, with him sporting a quiff and so on. His attention to detail was extraordinary. On the way back to London I scribbled my notes down on the back of a train ticket. This became the seeds of a PR plan.'

Beckham's footballing and commercial interests at that point were managed by agent Tony Stephens at SFX Management. Beckham, Victoria, Stephens, Edwards, lawyer Andrew Thompson and financial adviser Charles Bradbrook formed a tight team. 'Often a football agent wants to do the PR and control everything,' says Edwards. 'But Tony was very open to the brand being developed. He just let us get on with the PR strategy.' Reporting to Edwards at Outside Organisation, and increasingly working closely with Beckham, was the young Caroline McAteer, who came to be known as 'the rottweiler' in pursuing Beckham's interests.

But according to Edwards, much of the strategy in those days came from Beckham himself. 'David's approach towards self-improvement was two-fold. On the pitch he trained harder, worked harder, than everyone else. And second, it was about style; he was acutely conscious of the way he looked and was very original in that sense. He wasn't copying the other players at the time. He was drawing influences from American rap music and beyond.'

This attitude led to an iconic moment in the building of Brand Beckham. In 1998 David went out to a restaurant dressed in a capped sleeve T-shirt and a sarong round his waist. The look divided opinion, with many admiring his 'metrosexuality', while the traditionalists from the football community were scathing. Speaking later to the *Daily Star* Beckham said: 'Maybe I've sometimes overstepped the mark with something that a footballer in the past wouldn't wear, and that's led to trends or people trying new things. Everyone should be allowed to be who they are and dress how they want.'

Front page of *The Sun*, 4 June 1998
Source Martin Gibbs, News Syndication

By now Brand Beckham was forming, and broadening its appeal. Edwards says the strategy wasn't written down but was very clear to all involved: 'We weren't checking progress against our objectives every day. It was all very informal. There was no briefing document and the meetings were often round someone's house, but we knew where we were going. It was a campaign of perpetual motion.'

In 1999 Beckham signed a long-term deal with PepsiCo and in July that year the Beckhams were due to be married. Unsurprisingly, it wasn't set to be an understated affair. The wedding was booked at a castle in Ireland and is said to have cost £500,000. In the run-up to the wedding Edwards was responsible for signing one of the most lucrative celebrity exclusives of all time, prompting spiralling costs in the magazine world thereafter.

Martin Townsend, the former editor of *OK!* magazine, had contacted Edwards, who was also Victoria's manager at the time, to bid £1 million for exclusive pictures of the wedding. This was on the orders of *OK!* owner Richard Desmond, who had heard rumours about a big money offer from *The Sun*. In an article in *The Guardian*, Townsend recalled: 'I got on the phone to Victoria's agent and said, "Alan, we really want this wedding and we're prepared to offer you £1 million", and he nearly fell off his seat.'

Edwards explains that he had tried to get hold of the Beckhams but they were on a flight to Los Angeles, so he signed the deal. 'Now, I'm not a mathematical genius,' he smiles wryly, 'but the only other offer had been for £120,000 so this looked worth signing. I eventually spoke on the phone to Victoria in LA the next day and explained the background to her. She said: "So I hope you signed the deal?!" I reckon I'd have been fired if I hadn't.'

OK! sold 1.5 million copies of that issue, four times normal weekly sales. And despite criticism in some quarters of 'nouveau-riche garishness' it was becoming clear that 'Posh and Becks' was a marketing match made in heaven. Meanwhile the value of the Premier League and Manchester United brands was growing thanks partly to stars such as David. He was building a loyal personal fan base prompting scenes of adulation when he arrived in Japan for the 2002 World Cup finals. 'This was a new merging of sports and entertainment celebrities,' says Edwards. 'It was like working for the new aristocracy, particularly in a post-Princess Diana era. I think we changed the thinking around celebrities and brands and even to a certain extent, British popular culture.'

But the scale of this personal branding operation was causing its own problems. Sir Alex Ferguson, Beckham's football manager and mentor, was becoming frustrated with what he saw as the 'distractions' in his star midfielder's life. In his 2013 *My Autobiography* Ferguson writes: 'David was the only player I managed who chose to be famous, who made it his mission to be known outside the game. He had offers that would make your mind boggle. He was making twice outside of football what we were paying him.'

This led to a major, and ultimately terminal, confrontation between the two in February 2003 following an FA Cup match at Old Trafford. After losing to Arsenal, Ferguson criticized Beckham for his lack of effort in front of the team. Beckham swore and Ferguson kicked a football boot that was lying on the floor, which shot up to hit Beckham in the eye. The next day Beckham appeared in public with an Alice band pulling his hair back to reveal the cut above his eye. It was clear that his days at the club were coming to an end.

SFX began negotiations with Real Madrid, the biggest club in Europe, for Beckham to join them. It would extend his brand internationally, with Real briefing that it would make them an immediate profit in replica shirt sales alone. Ferguson writes: 'On Wednesday 18 June 2003 we told the London Stock Exchange he would be joining Real Madrid for a fee of £24.5 million. David was 28. The news flashed around the world. It was one of those global moments for our club.'

Edwards admits that the PR operation was also coming under strain. 'It was a challenge simply in physical logistics. We were trying to cover music, football and fashion. There were by now lots of brands to promote – David, Victoria, the Spice Girls, even the UK as a whole – and lots of media to cover.'

Victoria, who wanted to develop the brand internationally, approached her former manager, Simon Fuller, a lifelong Manchester United supporter. He agreed to take on both Beckhams as clients and bought out the entire operation, including David's contract with Alan Edwards' Outside Organisation and the later contract with SFX. It was to become a key turning point in the story of Brand Beckham.

Phase 2 *August 2003 to May 2013*

In August 2003 Beckham signed a $160 million lifetime sponsorship contract with sportswear firm Adidas, earning nearly half the money upfront. The *Sunday Mirror* described it as 'the biggest commercial contract in the history of sport'. The size of his deals was now exceeding those of his sporting idols, Muhammad Ali and Michael Jordan. Beckham had three years remaining on his current deal, and Adidas's then global football executive, Thomas Van Schaik, said: 'David Beckham's global market appeal is unsurpassed and will extend beyond his playing days.'

Adidas' ambition for Beckham matched Simon Fuller's. With a new management contract in place Fuller began to construct a dedicated team of professionals around both Beckhams with the long-term aim of developing two separate businesses that could stand alone and exist as their own profit centres, under the single umbrella of 'Brand Beckham'. Fuller signed England and Chelsea physio Terry Byrne to become David's exclusive sports consultant, while 19's creative director Catri Drummond was given the role of helping Victoria develop her fledgling interest in fashion, and the 19 commercial team took on the management of the Beckham's sponsors.

For communication strategy Fuller turned to his trusted PR adviser Julian Henry, whose background as marketing agent to Coca-Cola and Disney brought a calm and structured approach to the plan, something Fuller was keen to use to lay the foundations of Brand Beckham. 'I've never believed in fame for the sake of it', Henry says. 'It was clear that we needed to start saying no to the media a lot more. We set David's personal publicist Caroline McAteer up in partnership to take care of his interests and to ensure that his creative instincts were given full rein. David trusted Caroline. It was important he had someone strong to ensure he was protected when he left SFX and Manchester United.'

Although Beckham was settling in well at Madrid, his new team at 19 Entertainment was distracted by claims made by the British newspaper, the *News of the World*. A sequence of stories brokered by the publicist Max Clifford threatened to blow Beckham's 'family man' image. The claims were later dismissed by Beckham's legal team at Harbottle & Lewis.

The negative publicity reminded the Beckham camp that not everyone wanted him to succeed in his new life in Spain, so while Henry and McAteer locked horns with the British press, Fuller took steps to restore the faith of the wider sports community in Beckham's standing by focusing on his role as an ambassador and inspiration for young talent. The first David Beckham Academy was launched in London and Los Angeles and young sports PR Simon Oliveira was hired to encourage the support of the football media. Oliveira's background at Ketchum and his experience on Adidas made him an ideal candidate for protecting Beckham's reputation from the rougher elements within the Fleet Street pack.

The new strategy paid dividends; David's football career started to settle down in Spain, and he was able to concentrate on his role as England captain. But Fuller had to continue to show the world that

Beckham was no ordinary sportsman and when the National Portrait Gallery revealed their new acquisition – a Sam Taylor Wood art exhibit which captured Beckham asleep – it reminded the world of the player's iconic appeal.

But by late 2006 Beckham had fallen out of favour with Real Madrid owner Ramon Calderón and, after long discussions, a key strategic decision was made that was to finally transform Brand Beckham into the international and blue-chip brand that it is today. In January 2007 Beckham had signed a five-year deal to play for Major League Soccer [MLS] club LA Galaxy beginning in July, meaning that the entire family would be relocating to Hollywood. It was a shock move because at that time Beckham was still only 31 and US soccer was not at the standard of European football. In a scathing speech in Spain, Calderón said that Beckham was 'going to Hollywood to be half a film star'.

Julian Henry remembers: 'We never saw it as a risk. We had complete belief in David and Victoria's desire to succeed in the States, and spent a year going back and forth to LA planning it, interviewing different staff and hammering out the options. Fuller eventually appointed Rogers & Cowan under Paul Bloch working alongside CAA to handle their arrival. Paul has repped Eddie Murphy, Travolta, Stallone, Bruce Willis and knows how to handle the big stars. David and Victoria were deadly serious and Fuller wanted absolute precision in our messaging and strategy so it was vital that we have the biggest gun in the cupboard.'

'It was a fight at first because soccer was still a new sport in America,' adds Henry. 'The MLS wasn't ready for a star of David's status. At that time sports journalists were allowed to just wander into the dressing room right after each match to chat to the players; there was no security. It was obvious that they didn't know what was about to hit them'.

The deal that Simon Fuller constructed with LA Galaxy and the MLS was groundbreaking, and not only because of its size (claimed to be worth over $250 million) but because it gave Beckham the opportunity to invest in the sport and profit from his work there long after his playing days were finished. Beckham's actual playing deal with Galaxy was a 5-year contract worth $32.5 million in total or $6.5 million per year, but with additional income from shirt sales and sponsorship it generated far more than that, the real value of the deal only emerging several years later at an investor convention in Hong Kong.

'I need to thank Simon Fuller for that bit of advice', Beckham said later when asked how his investment in Miami came about. 'It was Simon's idea to insert the clause back in 2007 with a right to buy a club that cheaply ($25 million), which isn't bad business considering the New York franchise has just gone for over $100 million'.

Meanwhile the PR charm offensive in the USA, masterminded by Fuller, Henry, Oliveira and Jo Milloy (a dedicated publicist recruited to represent Victoria Beckham and the family) swung into action. On the Beckhams' arrival in Los Angeles in July 2007 the airport was packed with reporters and paparazzi followed by a global press conference on the pitch of LA Galaxy. David was photographed for the covers of multiple magazines including *Sports Illustrated* and *Details*, and was shot by Stephen Klein with Victoria for the August 2007 issue of *W*. Victoria appeared on *The Tonight Show* with Jay Leno to talk about their move to LA, presenting Leno with a number 23 Galaxy jersey, the number that David would use, with his own name on the back.

Once in the United States, with the freedom of a less demanding football schedule, Beckham's charity initiatives and commercial deals reached a new level. He became an ambassador for UNICEF and a founding member of the Malaria No More UK Leadership Council, launching the charity in 2009 with Andy Murray at Wembley Stadium. Beckham also appeared in a 2007 public service announcement for Malaria No More in the US, advertising the need for inexpensive bed nets and conducted a youth clinic in Harlem, along with other current and former MLS players.

With the PR machinery now working overtime Fuller began to activate his commercial drive, establishing a series of companies with himself, David, and Victoria as equal partners. In 2007 they received a payment of $13.7 million to launch the fragrance line *Homme by David Beckham* in the USA. Other endorsements included Armani, Breitling, Diet Coke and Burger King. Fuller explains: 'A key reason why David's fame grew to such enormous scale all over the world was because we always chose to work with the world's strongest and most powerful corporate partners. Our decision making was never just about the money but more importantly about the creative marketing and the global profile that they provided.'

However, the end of David Beckham's first season in Los Angeles would best be described as 'chequered'. He suffered from a series of injuries and the team underperformed so when *Sports Illustrated* journalist Grant Whal published his book *The Beckham Experiment* some critics complained that he'd not had the impact that they'd expected in relation to his reward.

And yet he and 19 Entertainment still worked hard to maintain his good reputation and to continue developing the brand, both in the US and abroad. In May 2010 Oliveira took Beckham to Afghanistan in a morale-boosting visit to British troops there and in 2012, after winning the MLS league title with Galaxy, Beckham signed another two-year contract. After a successful term with Armani, Fuller's commercial team negotiated a partnership with Swedish retailer H&M for his own line of underwear, T-shirts and pyjamas, a truly global partnership that promotes the Beckham brand in over 3,500 stores in more than 50 countries around the world. The resultant advertising was stylish but raunchy and only enhanced Beckham's status as a sex symbol; but most importantly it was the first time David Beckham, through another canny Fuller negotiation, had a share in the business. The H&M campaign, along with his bestselling Coty Fragrance range, were the first true steps towards establishing a legitimate David Beckham-branded business.

When the 2012 Olympic Games were hosted near his birthplace in London, Beckham was chosen to deliver the torch to the opening event of the Games. As a big (and always unpaid) supporter of London's bid, a smiling Beckham was filmed live, driving a motor-boat down the River Thames, holding aloft the flaming torch. His standing in the UK had never been higher.

'David is a proud and passionate individual,' explains Fuller. 'And this is highlighted best when he has been committed to causes and interests beyond just the world of football. Whether this has been him helping to bring the Olympics to London, his work with

UNICEF, or generally supporting Britain as an ambassador around the world.'

When Beckham announced in late 2012 that he would be leaving LA Galaxy the following year *Forbes* estimated that he would have earned $255 million during his time in the US, just ahead of the ambitious target 19 Entertainment set in 2007. *Forbes* wrote:

> During Beckham's entire six years in Major League Soccer, the last two in which he won the league championship with the Galaxy, average attendance climbed each year. Part of this was due to the increase in the number of franchises (7), though MLS executives credited the expansion to the exposure Becks brought to their league. Last season, average attendance (18,800) eclipsed averages in the NBA (17,375) and the NHL (17,450). Additionally, television rights were sold to more than 130 countries.

In January 2013 Beckham signed a five-month deal to play his twilight football at Paris St Germain (PSG) and in a PR masterstroke, announced his entire salary during his time there would be donated to a Parisian children's charity. By May 2013 Beckham won a fourth different top-flight winners' medal after PSG claimed their national title. He immediately announced his retirement from professional football, at the age of 38.

At that time global brand valuation consultancy Brand Finance estimated that Beckham's retirement from football would actually see his branded earnings flourish, predicting that he could become a $500 million brand.

Postscript ...

Since retiring, Beckham and Fuller have continued to develop their interests in joint ventures that include equity stakes. In October 2013 it emerged that Beckham was keen to exercise his 2007 option to create a new MLS team for $25 million (franchises are usually sold for around $100 million) and that he and Fuller had chosen Miami for the initiative. It was one of the few major cities in the US without a strong football team despite its large Hispanic community. The team was due to start playing in 2017.

In 2014 Beckham and Fuller partnered with beverage company Diageo to launch a new single-grain Scotch whisky called Haig Club, with the Chinese market a major focus. Beckham and Fuller took a 50 per cent stake in the venture and worked with Diageo on strategy, positioning and advertising, which was handed to hot London ad agency Adam & Eve/DDB.

Later that year saw an even more ambitious deal with Hong Kong-based Global Brands Group, which owns Calvin Klein, Coach, Tommy Hilfiger and many Chinese brands. Beckham and Fuller took a 50 per cent stake in a joint venture that would develop Beckham-branded products across the world, in clothing and luxury products globally. Fuller and both Beckhams had already worked with Jaguar Land Rover in China and remain keen to target what is potentially the world's biggest consumer market.

But the focus on good PR continued to underpin Brand Beckham's interests on both sides of the Atlantic. In January 2014, he appeared on *Late Night with Jimmy Fallon* on NBC in America, and in March he made a guest appearance in the BBC's Sport Relief special of *Only Fools and Horses*, a classic British TV comedy.

Fuller says: 'Editorial media is of course essential and every opportunity is considered carefully. We have always made sure we had the best people around us to provide guidance all over the world. However, the most important thing is to make sure the media are interested in David and want to report favourably.'

ON REFLECTION

- While not a classic PR campaign, this is a personal marketing campaign underpinned by exceptional reputational management, encapsulating the classic communications-led formula of single-minded vision, strong strategy, tight executive team and rigorous management of narrative.

- Promotional communications were always energetic and brave, constantly extending Beckham's brand into new sectors, even countries. As with any high-profile figure or organization, there were challenging times, even occasional crises, but Beckham remained calm and focused throughout. As Fuller points out: 'They say that true greatness comes from how one is perceived during the great highs in a career as well as the great lows. David Beckham has a remarkable intuition for how to behave in those defining moments. David's humility and unswerving determination has been the main reason why he has become such a much loved, respected and iconic sportsman.'

- The wider impact of this campaign was to change the relationship between celebrity, talent and business. David and Victoria Beckham were among the first celebrities to blur the traditional lines that separated sport, fashion and entertainment. In the late 1990s they almost became a 'new royalty' in the eyes of the media. But 'Posh and Becks' developed this concept throughout the 2000s, embracing new types of commercial endorsements, tie-ups and ventures. By 2013 they were investigating how celebrity brands can leverage their value in joint-venture equity deals. Crucially, Beckham was able to move from a sponsorship model to an ownership model.

- It is best left to Simon Fuller to sum up: 'There are many great sports people, but few that transcend their sport. My focus in managing David's career has been to have him perceived as so much more than just a football player. It has paid off in grand style, especially now that he has ended his playing career. After all the hard work we put in, building David's popularity and stature in the worlds of fashion and lifestyle, we now have endless opportunities to build businesses in many different areas.'

Acknowledgement

Alex Ferguson: My autobiography (2013) Sir Alex Ferguson, published by Hodder & Stoughton

Chapter Six
Inspiring a Generation
London 2012 Olympic
Games – 2005–2012

Introduction

The 2012 Summer Olympics in Britain – formally the Games of the XXX Olympiad, but more commonly known as London 2012 – took place from 25 July to 12 August 2012. The organization responsible for overseeing the planning, development and communication of these ultimately triumphant Games was LOCOG (The London Organising Committee of the Olympic and Paralympic Games). It was jointly established by the UK Government's Department for Culture, Media and Sport (DCMS), the Mayor of London and the British Olympic Association. LOCOG worked closely with the publicly-funded Olympic Delivery Authority (ODA), which was responsible for infrastructure. For reasons of space this case study will focus on the Olympic Games only, excluding the Paralympic Games, which was another powerful, innovative campaign that is worthy of its own analysis at a later date.

Why the campaign shook the world

In a well-crafted speech to open the London 2012 Games, LOCOG chairman Lord Sebastian Coe ended with the immortal words: 'For

Jackie Brock-Doyle
Source *PRWeek*

every Briton, just as the competitors, this is our time! And one day we will tell our children and our grandchildren that when our time came, we did it right.' Fortunately, the London 2012 team rose to the occasion. The team oversaw a safe, colourful and widely acclaimed Olympic Games. More than that: against a high level of scepticism in many quarters, London's own image and reputation was significantly enhanced both nationally and globally and it created a new confidence across the UK.

Following the terrorist attacks on 7 July 2005, the day after London won the bid, there had been growing concern about the safety and social stability of the host-city-to-be. And this was heightened in August 2011, one year before the Games were due to begin, with extensive riots on London's streets. The notoriously aggressive British media were also questioning, right from day one, what the 'legacy' of the Games would be for the city, and for the wider nation.

In the aftermath of London 2012, however, the consensus was that the stakeholders had answered these concerns with aplomb. Thankfully it was to prove an Olympic Games with no major security incidents. Like any project of this type, legacy continues to be a contentious issue but, generally, the regeneration of the part of east London used for most of the events is accepted to have been successful and the stadiums will be put to future use.

Moreover, for TV viewers around the world, the view was that London 'simply looked great' thanks to a sporting and cultural event that was aesthetic and well staged. Few would now disagree that, in the end, Seb Coe and his team 'did it right'.

Why is the campaign great?

For such a long campaign – seven years from winning the bid to completion of the Games – there was laudable consistency and discipline in approach. Also notable was a talented and stable team, which CEO Paul Deighton always said was crucial to the campaign's 'authenticity'. He wanted everyone committed to the strategy, and emotionally involved from the beginning to the end.

The campaign achieved its main objective with distinction thanks to the crystal clarity of the vision from the early days. This led to an unusually high level of consensus on strategy and in the key messages delivered on the ground. Jackie Brock-Doyle, London 2012's director of communications and public affairs, points out: 'If you had asked anyone, at any point, from the Mayor of London to an athlete or a volunteer what was at the heart of this campaign, they would have replied "It's about inspiring the next generation".' Even the evaluation was professional and consistent, with monthly tracking on the same measures of public support. Although this inevitably oscillated, remarkably it rarely fell below 70 per cent throughout.

Inevitably there were crises. Indeed, at times the members of the team came under immense pressure, but overall morale and discipline remained high. All this was achieved in the face of sceptical British media, and under the restrictions of a tight and highly scrutinized financial budget. The London 2012 team was forced to work hard and efficiently, with the optimum use of marketing communications agency resources.

Finally, the campaign proved exemplary for its integration and innovation. London organizers were the first to manage an Olympic Games in the full glare of globalized social media. Digital communications became a bigger part of this campaign than even was originally envisaged. The London 2012 team was smart enough to learn quickly, implementing online solutions and products adeptly.

The cast

Lord Sebastian Coe (born 1956), executive chairman of LOCOG
'Seb' Coe was the figurehead and inspirational leader of the London 2012 campaign, as indeed he was of the bid that secured the Games for London in 2005. Coe came to fame as a middle-distance runner, winning Olympic Gold in the 1,500 metres in 1980 and 1984, but was to later reinvent himself as a politician, then as a major global player in sports administration and marketing.

Lord Sebastian Coe, 2011
Source Flickr/Foreign and Commonwealth Office

A highly-driven individual, Coe is also socially adept and a strong team player. When the London 2012 comms team won 'Campaign of the Year' and 'Team of the Year' at the *PRWeek* Awards 2012, to a spontaneous standing ovation, Coe turned up to applaud his team on to the stage. In 2007, he was elected a vice president of the International Association of Athletics Federations and in August 2011 re-elected for another four-year term. In 2012 he became chairman of the British Olympic Association and in 2013 he became an executive chairman of the London-based sports marketing agency Chime Sports Marketing. He is now also a director of the publicly-listed parent, Chime Communications.

Paul Deighton (born 1956), CEO of LOCOG – now Lord Deighton
The former COO of Goldman Sachs in London, Deighton was appointed chief executive officer of LOCOG in December 2005. The directors reported to Deighton and he sat on all the key committees. His successful stewardship of the operation was later rewarded with the Olympic Order by the IOC (International Olympic Committee). He was made a life peer on 1 November 2012 and received a KBE in January 2013. Soon afterwards Deighton became a junior minister in Prime Minister David Cameron's government with responsibility for implementing the National Infrastructure Plan and supporting the culture secretary with the ongoing 2012 Olympics legacy.

Jackie Brock-Doyle OBE, director of communications and public affairs (see Campaign Star below)
Brock-Doyle led a core comms team of 10 staff including **Joanna Manning-Cooper** (head of PR and media), **Nicky Hughes** (head of government relations) and **Alex Balfour** (head of new media), and used a network of PR agencies including Hill + Knowlton (international), Freuds (torch relay), Pitch (ticketing) and Edelman (logo and licensing products).

Other key members of LOCOG
Sir Keith Mills (deputy chair), **Debbie Jevans OBE** (director of sport), **Terry Miller OBE** (general counsel), **Chris Townsend** (commercial director), **Chris Denny** (head of marketing), **Greg Nugent** (director of brand, marketing and culture from May 2009), **Jonathan Edwards** (representing athletes), **James Bulley OBE** (director of venues and infrastructure), **Charles Allen** (nations and regions group).

Other key players
Tessa Jowell MP (culture secretary, then minister for London until 2010), **Boris Johnson** (mayor of London from May 2008), **Hugh Robertson** (sports minister), **Deborah Hale MBE** (torch relay producer).

★ THE CAMPAIGN STAR ★
Jackie Brock-Doyle

London 2012 was far from a one-off for Brock-Doyle. She had been instrumental in communicating the Sydney 2000 Olympic Games through Australian consultancy Capital PR, and had subsequently advised major sporting events around the world. In 2002 she was parachuted in to help out the Commonwealth Games in Manchester that year, as director of marketing and communication. Brock-Doyle applied her no-nonsense approach immediately: 'I asked the Manchester leaders what their vision was, and they replied: "Well, that's your job isn't it?" So I told them in no uncertain terms that their job was to set the vision, mine was to tell the world about it.' The 2002 Commonwealth Games were ultimately a media and public success story that helped pave the way for Britain's Olympic bid.

In May 2003 Brock-Doyle was hired by then culture secretary Tessa Jowell to work on London's bid for the 2012 Games. Jowell wanted to get the 'warring fiefdoms' involved to work better together and to stem the flow of media leaks. Brock-Doyle, working with Keith Mills, Seb Coe and director of comms Mike Lee, helped secure a winning bid for London.

Born in 1965 Brock-Doyle is tough, disciplined and straight-talking in her approach. She knows her own mind and claims to need only four or five hours of sleep a night, which was useful bearing in mind she managed to get an average of three each night during the Games. She is also known for her colourful use of language and an ability to fight her corner with tough journalists. That said, her staff attest to her approachability and sense of humour.

At London 2012 it was Brock-Doyle who chaired the vital Communications and Engagement Committee, on which all the marketing chiefs sat. And crucially everything that was said about the Games came through that committee. Brock-Doyle also had a place on all the other key committees from 2008 onwards.

Coe and Deighton, to whom Brock-Doyle is fiercely loyal, acknowledge her as pivotal in the project's success. She attributes this to remaining focused on 'the end game not just the journey'. She explains: 'I had been through the Sydney Olympic Games and the Manchester Commonwealth Games and had been at the pointy, sharp end before, where it can be terrifying. All of these memories reminded me to keep asking ourselves: "For what are they going to hold you accountable when it comes to Games time?"'

Brock-Doyle has not always been consumed by the sporting world. She began her career in 1984 with the outstanding PR consultancy of the time, Paragon Communications, before becoming head of corporate comms at retail group Kingfisher from 1992 to 1995. 'My love of campaigning began when I was at Kingfisher,' says Brock-Doyle. 'We lobbied the Government on the regulation of everything from Sunday trading to perfume sales and CD pricing.'

Brock-Doyle was named *PRWeek*'s 'PR Professional of the Year' for 2012 and went on to receive an OBE in January 2013. She is regularly named as the most powerful woman in the British PR industry. At the time of writing Brock-Doyle is chairman of Good Relations, the PR division of Chime Communication, where she continues to work, alongside the sports division's chairman Seb Coe, on major events worldwide and corporate clients.

THE CAMPAIGN

London 2012 bid hit by backlash

LONDON'S TORCH GOES OUT

Denis Campbell explains why even those in charge of the capital's bid for the 2012 Olympic Games privately concede that Paris will win

London's Olympic dream in tatters

● Key British officials admit Paris 'will win'
● Lack of funds for sport drains IOC support

London's Olympic bid suffers blow

Newspaper coverage
Source Jackie Brock-Doyle, LOCOG strategy team

The context

On 6 July 2005, after a tough three-year bidding process, London narrowly won the bid to host the 2012 Olympics, prompting national elation. Sadly this was to prove short-lived. The following day, now known as '7/7', British-born Muslim suicide bombers murdered 52 civilian passengers on London's transport system. The incident prompted concerns nationally and internationally about whether London could host a safe and secure Olympic Games.

Second, sceptics questioned the sustainability of the whole enterprise. The two previous Games at that point – Sydney 2000 and Athens 2004 – had been left with unused infrastructure, some falling into dereliction, at a high cost to the public.

It all added to complex politics at LOCOG. Brock-Doyle recalls, 'When we won the bid to host the Games and had signed the contract with the BOA (British Olympic Authority) and the British Government, the priority was to implement the rules of engagement

we had drawn up in the bid. While you're bidding, government partners tend to support but once you've won they all think they should
be running it. Suddenly people are land-grabbing and not always
the bits they should.'

The objective

A successful Olympic Games that would inspire a generation.

The strategy

The London 2012 communications strategy had three strands:

- **Basics** – ensure solid foundations to build confidence in the
  project: from the building and the staging, to the athletes'
  preparation and legacy planning. 'These were designed to
  provide the heartbeat of the project,' says Brock-Doyle.
  'We told people what we would do, we told them we were
  doing it and we told them when we had done it.'

- **Bringing the Games to life** – create a series of high-profile
  activities that would generate excitement and engage the
  attention of the media, the public and other stakeholders.
  These would include annual countdown events, ticket sales, a
  nationwide Join In campaign, the torch relays and the opening
  ceremony.

- **What we want the world to remember** – focus on the five
  themes that originally drove the winning bid: the engagement
  of young people; the transformation of east London; inspirational
  sport and athletes; London as the place to be; and a Games
  that are accessible to everyone. 'All media releases, speeches,
  photos, videos, events were tagged to one of these themes and
  regularly reviewed to make sure all the themes were effectively
  being communicated,' says Brock-Doyle.

How the narrative unfolded ...

Phase 1 *Summer 2005 to 2007*

The formative LOCOG team spent the first six months working out who was ultimately responsible for delivering what and agreeing a vision. Brock-Doyle explains, 'Because this was soon after the 7/7 London bombings, the original vision slide had the phrase "safe and secure Games" right in the middle. We realized we couldn't do that. Safety should of course be a hygiene factor rather than a brand promise. So later, Chris Denny (head of marketing) and I revisited the bid document and instead decided to focus on the five points that we had originally campaigned on. We recognized that in seven years' time those were the questions that would be asked of us. Seb (Coe) had always made the point that we had to keep telling people why we were hosting the Games not just how we were going to do it.'

From that point onwards the team focused on how to better engage young people and how to use the power of sport to inspire lasting change. This was the basis of the core mission statement: 'To inspire a generation'. 'We wanted to be both brave and authentic' says Brock-Doyle. 'In my experience marketing people have a tendency to want something new and fresh all the time, but to me it was important to focus on this simple strategy throughout. We would not claim to eradicate poverty, but we would give people, particularly young people, the opportunity to choose sport. So even when we took the inevitable flak along the way, they could never say we weren't delivering on what we promised.'

Brock-Doyle was keen to set the rules of engagement for the media. She wanted an open, equitable approach based on bringing all the editors onside: 'Everyone told me at the beginning you have to do media partnerships but with so many British newspaper groups, I decided we couldn't do that. The challenge was to work with each of them to create ideas that individual titles could own without alienating the others.'

The team also set out a consistent campaign 'narrative' based around events, stories and images, creating visual 'storyboards' for reference: 'Once you have the story you then pick the channels, the platforms. Not enough people take this approach, even today. All through the six years we tagged every story, every photo to one of our five key narratives.'

Brock-Doyle was personally determined to buck the typical trends in public support. In previous Olympic Games she had noticed that support tends to follow the same curves, with slumps in public popularity around four years before the event. 'Early on I said we were going to change the way people think. So we did lots of stuff to sell the Games to the country. We had lots of regional events. We had a bus, a roadshow and a Nations & Regions Group to help us. For two years we tried to explain how people around country could get involved and get them excited.' This drive for nationwide support was to prove crucial, as the campaign hit a difficult patch.

By the end of 2006 media stories arose of how the cost of hosting the Games was likely to almost quadruple, from £2.4 billion originally, to around £9 billion. 'The funding question was a complex one and we took a lot of flak,' admits Brock-Doyle. 'It took me about a month to explain to all our stakeholders that this cost story would be with us right until the end. Our approach was to avoid getting angry and to just explain. It actually ended up playing to our strengths because we decided to set a target for the whole project that over 90 per cent of Olympic contracts would go to businesses. In the end we let £6 billion of contracts – 96 per cent went to British business.'

In June 2007, the team thought it had a story to raise excitement – the launch of the official logo – but the reaction was distinctly underwhelming. 'Some of us are still receiving counselling,' jokes Brock-Doyle. The brightly coloured, jagged-edged logo was created by well-known branding consultancy Wolff Olins and signed off by the LOCOG board. Unfortunately only the outline and core colours could be unveiled publicly because the intellectual property (IP) needed to be robust as this was the core asset for the sponsors and we needed to raise £2 billion. Brock-Doyle takes up the story: 'Seb and I took the logo storyboards round a number of editors in advance and explained how it would develop. They loved it but said we must release the whole thing. However, doing that could risk the IP and we could not afford that. At the launch, in Camden's Roundhouse to 200 people, Seb unveiled the logo to a stony silence.'

The media reaction the next day was damning. One newspaper had asked a child, a blind person and a monkey to design an alternative logo, all of which it claimed were superior. Many accused the design of resembling a swastika – not great when Seb's first overseas speech was in Israel. Within four days of the launch nearly 50,000 people had signed the petition to change the logo. Eventually however the originator of the online petition took it down because although he hated the logo, he loved sport and the Games and was worried it was doing too much damage.

'We learned a lot from the logo launch,' says Brock-Doyle. 'It was a top-five story across the world for three days, but then it died down. We decided that we should hold tight and take the long view. The value of the logo at that stage was to attract £2 billion of sponsorship – it was all we had to offer them, so it needed to be protected. This is the reality that comms can bring to a campaign, you have to distinguish real risk from perceived risk.'

Phase 2 *2008 to summer 2012*

By early 2008 the team was planning for that year's Beijing Olympic Games which would set up the four-year run-in to the London Games, prompting it to embark on Phase 2 of the communications strategy, which was designed to build excitement at a time when there is traditionally a slump in public support (see Figure 6.1).

'We had two aims from Beijing: that our athletes would do well, not really in our gift; and that we would learn from an operational and media point of view,' explains Brock-Doyle. She took a group of British media to the rehearsals for the Beijing closing ceremony, where London was putting on a handover segment during the show. 'It helped us effectively bring the British media into our team,' she explains. At the same time, back home, LOCOG organized a big party on The Mall in London to mark the run-up to London's Olympics. Fortunately British athletes also did well in Beijing, coming fourth in the medals table (compared with tenth in Athens 2004).

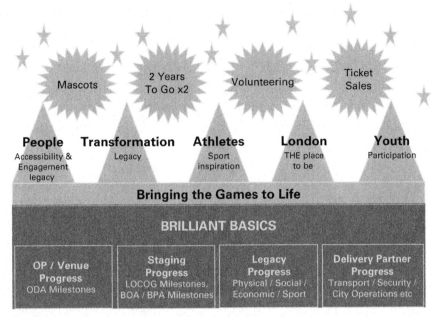

Figure 6.1 LOCOG communications strategy in 2010
Source Jackie Brock-Doyle

The next major 'event' for the team was to launch volunteering, which they did on the back of the 10-year anniversary of Sydney's Games. Seb Coe, surrounded by Sydney volunteers (a benchmark in sports volunteers) in Sydney Olympic Park, hit the morning news programmes in 2010. Around a quarter of a million people applied for the 70,000 places and they became a human symbol for a renewed British reputation when the Games came around.

A year later tickets went on sale, always a major challenge for the host nation because one must balance the need to sell out all events, while coping with the fact that some people will inevitably miss out on tickets and be disappointed.

'We didn't really have the budget for TV marketing and did most of the communications through PR,' admits Brock-Doyle. So for six months in the run-up to March 2011 the comms team planned the daily stories that would drive this PR campaign for a six-week period of the sale. 'It was sheer shoe leather. For 40 days we did a roadshow of local radio and local papers. We set up a media war-room at head office. People have forgotten how to do campaigning like that.'

With the backing of some outdoor advertising by McCann, the comms team used a combination of PR agencies Freuds and Pitch to help with this mini-campaign. A three-week social media drive was pivotal. Inevitably, when there were website problems due to sheer volume of last-minute hopefuls and some people failed to get tickets, the flak again hit LOCOG. But within the timeframe the operation managed to sell out all events, totalling 11 million tickets. Brock-Doyle: 'We were then accused of over-marketing it. And yet previously the stories had been that we wouldn't be able to sell tickets to some sports, which we did. Our aim was always to deliver to the biggest fans, those that most wanted to be there, and young people in particular.'

The next landmark was May 2012, when the Olympic torch arrived in Britain for an 80-day national tour before going to the new stadium in London. Marketing expert Deborah Hale was employed as torch relay producer to focus on the design, development and delivery of this tour, which took two years to plan and a dedicated team of 100 people. The route was developed so that 95 per cent of the UK population was within 10 miles of it. The dedicated torch campaign was called 'Moment to Shine' with more than half of the 8,000 torchbearers aged 16–25 and all with inspiring, humbling personal stories.

'We had some core principles and made some tough choices. We decided it was about local heroes and not about celebrities,' explains Brock-Doyle, who famously turned down an offer from Brad Pitt and Angelina Jolie to carry the flame. The comms team, supported by agency Freuds, did an exhausting media relations tour to support the relay, with the aim of making the torchbearers into local heroes beforehand and working closely with local councils. 'We did morning, lunchtime and evening celebrations, with different bearers, timed for the various broadcast news bulletins,' says Brock-Doyle. She recalls the first, emotionally charged day: 'We flew in from Athens on the British Airways "flame plane". I was sitting with Seb Coe, David Beckham and Tessa Jowell. As we came in to land we saw that thousands of people were there, with cars stopped on the road, watching us. We all turned to each other and mouthed 'Oh ... my ... God ...'.

A webcam (branded 'torchcam') was placed on the back of the bus, thanks to the BBC, to screen the whole relay live online. It meant that people could see the torch coming into their town and then stay connected after it had left. By the end of the tour 15 million people had turned out to see the flame live.

But another crisis was just around the corner. On July 11, two weeks before the Games were due to begin, the official security services provider for London 2012, G4S, admitted to ministers that it would not be able to deliver the numbers of security personnel it had promised. The next day defence secretary Philip Hammond was forced to announce that up to 3,500 extra troops would be needed for security duties during the Games.

LOCOG and the Government sought to reassure the public that there was 'no question of Olympic security being compromised' as a result. 'The G4S crisis was another big lesson for us,' says Brock-Doyle. 'Operationally we already had back-up of military. But the challenge was to support and motivate the 4,000 G4S people already working for us in the face of intense media criticism and international concern.' In the end the involvement of the British soldiers on duty contributed hugely to London 2012's atmosphere. Not only did their presence reassure the public but they proved a friendly addition to the volunteers present.

The Games were launched on 27 July 2012 with a now legendary opening ceremony directed by British film director Danny Boyle and electronic music by Underworld. It involved a cast of professional performers and 7,500 volunteers. Brock-Doyle talks of the challenges from a comms perspective. Such a huge cast and the operational need to have two dress rehearsals with a full stadium audience meant potential leaks which would have ruined the impact of the quirky show. 'We convinced Danny Boyle and the ceremonies team to work with social media rather than ban it. We came up with the hashtag #SaveTheSurprise. At both dress rehearsals Danny stood up in front of the stadium audience and asked them: "By all means tell people that you're here and what you think of the show but please don't divulge the details of the show, save the surprise". Only three pictures appeared and the Twittersphere quickly made them take their posts down. This is something you rarely see in the comms world. When you enable people, they can pay back your trust.'

Simultaneously marketing director Greg Nugent rallied local community leaders to hold opening ceremony parties right across the country.

British magazine *Q* perfectly summed up the public and media reaction to Boyle's opening ceremony. 'It could all have been so different. As the London 2012 summer Olympics approached, the tide of scepticism seemed almost irreversible. It took less than four hours on the night of Friday 27 July to turn the whole country around. Not only was the ceremony demonstrably not "sh*te", it was the most surprising, moving, spectacular cultural event this country had ever seen ... modern Britain, in all its berserk, multi-faceted glory.'

But of course the Games themselves still required an intensive comms operation. Each day Brock-Doyle got up at 5am and did her first conference call at 5.45am then she accompanied Coe, Deighton and Jevans for a daily meeting with the IOC. At 10am she chaired a daily global press conference. Brock-Doyle generally got to bed at 2am after signing off the *Village* newspaper. The comms teams worked in shifts around the clock. 'We were a machine of information. But our whole philosophy was one of partnership with the media. My advice to all spokespeople was that they had to view the press in front of them as friends, not foes, at all times.'

Issues and crisis planning was crucial in such a huge national event and involved a large operational room run by LOCOG with staff from the Government and the Metropolitan Police. 'This was tough,' admits Brock-Doyle. 'You are permanently paranoid about security issues. You are sitting in a bunker when everyone else is outside enjoying the Games. There were issues every day, most of which were relatively minor and never became public. The comms role was to monitor social media and triage the issues as they came in, working closely with all our partners.'

In the early days, the comms team had to deal with one TV station accusing 2012 of allowing too many empty seats at the smaller events. It was difficult for LOCOG because it could not re-sell tickets if people arrived late. But it made an announcement that it was releasing selected seats to local schools.

Press Conference, 27 July 2012
Source Getty Images: Jeff J Mitchell/Staff

This problem soon disappeared as the Games gathered momentum. On 4 August, now known as Super Saturday, British athletes won gold medals in six different events and many on prime time television. The nation, and the world, was by now enraptured.

By the close of the Olympic Games, British athletes achieved third place in the overall medals table and the public had been awed by the sport and the spectacle. The closing ceremony drew a global audience of hundreds of millions around the world, with the Spice Girls' surprise appearance proving the most tweeted moment of the whole Olympics, which had attracted 4 million tweets throughout.

Postscript ...

LOCOG's research immediately following the Games showed the extent to which it had met its main objectives. In terms of inspiring youth, 70 per cent of people believed children now felt more positive about sport. Some 83 per cent said the Games had been 'impressive and the country could be proud', while 80 per cent believed London 2012 'had improved the global image of London and the UK.'

Polls in summer 2013, a year after the Games had completed, discovered that public attitude was still supportive despite the euphoria wearing off. The proportion of the British public that would welcome the Games back to Britain was 74 per cent, while 70 per cent believed that 2012 'was still having a positive effect on the national mood'. In terms of the positive effect on encouraging more people to play sport in Britain, 83 per cent agreed with this, rising to 94 per cent among 18–24 year olds.

ON REFLECTION

- The stable and professional team LOCOG put in place, particularly the vision and leadership of Sebastian Coe and Paul Deighton, was essential to the success of this campaign.

- What really stands out from this case study is the ambition, clarity and consistency of the vision; a vision that truly connected with people, nationally and internationally.

- London 2012 was the first modern Olympics not to be screened via any commercial TV station in the host country. LOCOG's commercial team and the sponsors had to work more creatively on their content, resulting in a wealth of grassroots and regional programmes from sponsors.

- The campaign was also characterized by the team's constructive attitude to the media, viewing journalists as allies. In her typically direct style, Jackie Brock-Doyle explains her theory: 'If you treat the media as your enemy, they become the enemy and, frankly, you're f***ed. But treat them as partners of your comms team, and it becomes a very different sort of relationship. You don't always agree but there is joint respect.'

- Brock-Doyle and her team discovered an important truth: that the difference between what the public reads in newspapers, and what they actually think, is getting wider. In other words, unlike the early 1990s, just because you get bad press doesn't mean that the public doesn't support you.

- Significantly, London 2012 was the first social media Olympic Games. There were at the time 5 billion mobile phones in circulation and 350 million tweets every day; Facebook alone boasted 900 million monthly active users. As a result LOCOG needed to deliver 77 products, sites or services during the campaign. It gained 5 million social media followers from 201 countries.

- From an evaluation point of view, the team used monthly public opinion tracking research right throughout the campaign. Crucially, they continued to ask the public: 'Do you support the Games? Will they be good for the country?' And, through thick and thin, that public support rarely sank below 70 per cent.

Part Three
Modern marketing movements with digital convergence and purpose

Chapter Seven
Product (RED)
How Bono changed cause marketing – 2006–2014

Introduction

(RED) is a successful and global 'cause marketing' campaign that has raised hundreds of millions of dollars to fight AIDS in Africa. It involves an intriguing mix of celebrities and corporations in ambitious coalition. And it has created a new model for corporate social responsibility (CSR) campaigns.

Why the campaign shook the world

At the time of writing (RED), which was launched in January 2006, has raised over $300 million for The Global Fund to Fight AIDS, Tuberculosis and Malaria, an international financing institution that gives grants to combat these three diseases.

Prior to the creation of (RED), the vast majority of the money contributed to The Global Fund – set up as a public–private partnership in 2002 – had come from governments such as the US, UK, France and Germany. Indeed when (RED) launched, such governments had already given nearly $5 billion, but the private sector had contributed only $5 million. The great achievement of (RED) was to bring corporates and brands fully into the war against these devastating diseases, particularly in Africa, both in terms of funding and public awareness.

Matthew Freud
Source Matthew Freud

The campaign also galvanized A-list celebrities and politicians worldwide – from Oprah Winfrey and Kate Moss to Desmond Tutu – to contribute their time and image rights to raising public awareness of these issues. Few consumers worldwide would have been unaware of (RED) or untouched by the messages of this ambitious project.

(RED) was actually a powerful new addition to a 20-year movement that Microsoft founder Bill Gates coined 'conscious consumerism' and whose corporate incarnation is best described as 'cause marketing' (see The wider context on p 141). (RED) was to prove a game changer because for the first time it enabled companies to use cause-related marketing as mainstream marketing rather than occasional philanthropy. Moreover, it established an accepted formula for cause-related marketing, which was eventually adopted by corporations around the world.

Why is the campaign great?

(RED) was groundbreaking because it provided a solution to the tricky conundrum of matching corporate capitalism with civic causes via the charity sector. Matthew Freud describes it in typically colourful terms: '(RED) invented a condom that allowed safe sex between companies and charities; a completely transparent relationship between product purchase and charity donation to a particular cause.'

Consumers could be encouraged to buy certain products on the basis that a certain percentage of their purchase fee would go directly to a specified good cause. The mechanics were set out as upfront and honest and the charity delivery process set up to be transparent and first-class.

From the outset of the (RED) project there was no capital investment, and no overheads were charged. All the money from products goes directly to The Global Fund to finance HIV programmes in Africa. In this sense it was a movement that became a campaign, which in turn became a large-scale movement. Significantly, it was a new type of complex coalition between brands, celebrities, politicians and consumers that changed the thinking of marketing departments around the globe, both within corporations and NGOs.

We will also see that as the campaign developed, thanks to the influence of British PR agency Freuds, the emphasis of earned media and events (PR) really helped drive the brand's success.

The cast

Bono, co-founder

The U2 vocalist is best known as one of the globe's biggest rock stars and an outspoken campaigner. Freud alternatively describes Bono as 'one of the great global marketeers and world's greatest popular communicator'. This may be overstating the case but there is little doubt that the Dublin-born singer is far from the typical rock 'n' roll flash-in-the-pan talent.

Bono presenting the (RED) credit card
Source Getty Images: Eric Bouvet/Contributor

Born in 1960, Bono participated in the seminal Band Aid charity single back in 1985 and has been a renowned businessman, philanthropist and activist ever since. Two decades later it was his vision, open-mindedness and relentless energy that proved the real power behind (RED). Those close to him say that, despite his vast portfolio of interests, (RED) and his campaigning around global health remains second only to U2 in his list of personal priorities.

Bobby Shriver, co-founder

Shriver, born in 1954, had worked with Bono on founding advocacy organizations DATA (Debt, AIDS, Trade, Africa) and the ONE campaign. A nephew of John F Kennedy, Shriver was the first CEO of (RED). The attorney-turned-film producer, and latterly mayor of Santa Monica, is legendary for his drive, charm and political networking.

Sheila Roche

The less public face of the campaign behind (RED) but instrumental since the early days of 2005. Roche is the former deputy manager of U2 who has been on the ground with Bono and Shriver from day one. As chief creative and communications officer, Roche has consistently been involved in the brand's creative strategy and is behind (RED)'s record-breaking art auctions and music events.

Bill Gates

The Microsoft founder could eventually go down in history as the greatest global philanthropist. The Bill & Melinda Gates Foundation has been a key partner of The Global Fund from the beginning. At the time of writing the foundation had pledged a total of $1.6 billion to the NGO. The foundation also provided additional support for (RED) specifically. Microsoft, when Gates was still chairman, signed up as one of (RED)'s first partners and Gates personally appeared in promotional events for the wider campaign, including its launch.

★ **THE CAMPAIGN STAR** ★

Matthew Freud

Born in 1963, Freud is one of the seminal figures of the modern PR industry. This is appropriate considering his family background. His great-grandfather was the father of psychoanalysis Sigmund Freud and he is also related to the 'father' of public relations, Edward Bernays (whose mother was Sigmund Freud's sister). The later generations remain distinguished: Matthew is the nephew of the late artist Lucian Freud and the son of the late Liberal MP Sir Clement Freud. Matthew's sister, Emma Freud OBE, is a broadcaster and the partner of film director and Comic Relief founder Richard Curtis CBE.

But Freud has managed to emerge from the shadow of his family as independently entrepreneurial. He set up his own PR consultancy, Freuds, in 1985 at the tender age of 22. He subsequently sold it to, and then bought it back from, two marketing services groups – Abbott Mead Vickers BBDO and Publicis. At the time of writing Freuds is once again independent, remains a top-10 UK consultancy with several hundred staff, and enjoys an annual turnover of £30 million. An attempt to take Freuds international a decade ago, with fledgling offices in New York and Los Angeles, petered out however.

PepsiCo is a longstanding client and Freud became famous in the 1990s for a stunt in which he arranged for Concorde to be painted blue in order to raise awareness of Pepsi's brand colour change. The successful campaign also involved a photo-call with supermodel Claudia Schiffer. Freuds has also long advised BSkyB, KFC, Mars and the BAFTAs, as well being instrumental in the London 2012 Olympics campaign. The agency has always been a curious mix of high-level strategic consultancy (from Freud himself and a few senior advisers) and professional party and event organizers. This balance gives Freud both gravitas and showbiz value.

Freud is most famous, however, for his ability to network with the great and the good, and for his ability to form effective, profitable coalitions. Previously married to Rupert Murdoch's daughter, Elisabeth, the couple's parties were legendary with Tony Blair and Rebekah Brooks regularly rubbing shoulders with Kate Moss and Simon Cowell. However, tension with the Murdoch family, which Freud helped to establish in London 'society', grew at the time of the phone-hacking scandal in 2011 (see Britain's phone-hacking scandal, p 71) and the couple separated in 2014. Their house in Primrose Hill, where Freud still lives, is a combination of family home, Hollywood-style personal 'office' and the perfect party venue. This house, in a mews in one of central London's most elegant neighbourhoods, hosts art from family friends including Damien Hirst and Gilbert & George. Freud confides that he never invites photographers to his legendary house parties because they are just that – private parties: 'I have made friends with a lot of interesting, talented people over the years and I want them to relax.'

In person, Freud defies the caricature. Although confident and astute, he is shy, serious and with notable intellectual heft. He is obsessive about business, the media and brands and will happily talk for hours on communications theory.

Today Freud says he is most proud of the work that his firm has contributed to cause-related campaigns such as Comic Relief, Make Poverty History and (RED). He is highly motivated by his pivotal role in campaigns that have successfully allied senior politicians, celebrities, brands and NGOs – very much the Matthew Freud milieu. In popular culture Freud's image will remain that of a (slightly oxymoronic) secretive socialite. For the marketing and media world he is more usefully viewed as a successful agency entrepreneur, an innovator and someone with unique insight into the fascinating nexus where politics, business and celebrity collide.

THE CAMPAIGN

The wider context of 'conscious consumerism' and 'cause marketing'

(RED) can only be properly understood in the broader context of the popular movement, which emerged fully in the 1980s, to get the Western world to do more about poverty and disease in poorer countries.

In the mid-1980s, rock musicians Bob Geldof (originally with the Boomtown Rats) and Midge Ure (Ultravox) were so dismayed by the devastating famine in Ethiopia, and the lack of help forthcoming from 'first-world' countries, that they launched first a charity single 'Band Aid' (Christmas 1984) and then a charity concert 'Live Aid' on both sides of the Atlantic (summer 1985). These were the first signs of a concept in the Western world that could best be described as 'conscious consumerism' – a phrase coined by Microsoft founder Bill Gates – or 'ethical consumerism', which encourages consumers to pay for things they love anyway, but with a 'good cause' as the ultimate beneficiary. In the same year, and also in response to famine in Africa, the comedy scriptwriter Richard Curtis and comedian Lenny Henry set up a British charity called Comic Relief. This charity developed quickly and today states that it exists 'to bring about positive and lasting change in the lives of poor and disadvantaged people ... as well as tackling the root causes of poverty and injustice'. The highlight of Comic Relief's appeal is Red Nose Day, a biennial telethon held in March, now alternating with sister project Sport Relief. By March 2015, Comic Relief announced that over its 30 years of operation it had raised over £1 billion for good causes.

Comic Relief logo
Source Comic Relief

▶

Alongside these charity fundraisers an additional element developed to involve businesses in this movement. This can best be described as 'cause marketing'. One of the fundamental principles behind working at Comic Relief is the 'golden pound principle' where every single donated pound sterling is spent on charitable projects. All operating costs, such as staff salaries, are covered by corporate sponsors or interest earned on money waiting to be distributed. Indeed, one-third of all the money raised by Comic Relief has been raised through its corporate partners including telecoms firm BT, the Sainsbury's supermarket chain and British Airways.

Twenty years on from Live Aid and the first Comic Relief, Geldof and Curtis – and U2's Bono – linked up to create the Live 8 music concerts as part of that year's Make Poverty History (MPH) campaign. The aim of MPH was to increase awareness of extreme poverty and pressure governments into taking action towards ending it. The symbol of the campaign was a product: a white 'awareness bracelet' made of cotton or silicone, which three million people were encouraged to buy as a donation. The precise aims of MPH were 'trade justice' with poor countries, dropping their unpayable debts, and 'more and better aid'. None of these aims were new but the scale of the 2005 campaign dwarfed previous efforts. For the Live 8 entertainment element, Geldof, Curtis and friends managed to convince Madonna, Robbie Williams and many more superstars to perform concerts in London, Paris, Rome, Berlin and Philadelphia.

The aim was to influence the decisions that would be made when the heads of the G8 countries met in Scotland the following week. Curtis said at the time: 'I haven't done anything to attempt to affect government decisions before, but it's just got to be worthwhile. Bob Geldof told me that by having tea with President Mitterrand of France he probably made more money for Africa than from the whole of Live Aid.'

MPH represented a fascinating new type of coalition between NGOs, religious groups, trade unions and celebrities, who mobilized around Britain's prominence in world politics (2005 was the year when Britain held the presidency of both the European Union and the G8 alliance of nations). Some viewed Live 8 as a huge success, including Bob Geldof himself. Chris Martin of Coldplay described Live 8 as 'the greatest thing that's probably been organized ever in the history of the world'. Others, however, slammed it for being a mere publicity stunt that had diverted media attention away from other elements of Make Poverty History such as a mass march. Tragically, public attention was quickly diverted away by the London bombings on 7 July, the day after Live 8 Edinburgh, the final concert in the series. When the G8 summit concluded on 8 July, the leaders pledged to increase aid to developing countries by US$50 billion overall by 2010, including an increase of US$25 billion in aid for Africa.

Nevertheless MPH set the stage for the corporate world to make a bigger contribution to this by-now powerful movement. The world economy was booming in the mid-2000s with record corporate profitability. The question was whether businesses could tap into this concept of conscious consumerism and contribute an amount equivalent to a national government in the fight against poverty and disease. This is where (RED) came in.

Bob Geldof promotes Live8
Source Getty Images: Tiziana Fabi/Stringer

The context

The year (RED) came about, 2005, was one of heightened consumer activism. The Make Poverty History campaign had launched in Great Britain and Ireland. And this activism was increasingly mirrored around the globe. In April 2005 a commercial aired in the United States with several celebrities in a black and white video stating the pledge of the American ONE Campaign – the US version of Make Poverty History. Founded by U2 vocalist Bono and activist, attorney and journalist Bobby Shriver, the ONE TV commercial featured 33 celebrities including the singer P Diddy and actors Brad Pitt, Susan Sarandon and Tom Hanks. The general goals of the ONE campaign in the United States were to end extreme poverty, hunger and AIDS. The founding sponsors of ONE included the NGOs DATA, Oxfam America and World Vision.

DATA and ONE had been key advocates for government funding for The Global Fund to Fight AIDS, Tuberculosis and Malaria. The Global Fund had been set up as a public–private partnership in 2002, and by 2005 had raised $5 billion from governments – but the contribution from the private sector was comparatively tiny, at $5 million. Importantly, governments were not willing to give any more state funding until the private sector contributed more. The idea behind (RED) was to get corporations to step up to the plate, with the added advantage of their growing political influence. Bono consistently made the point that (RED) was as important in its awareness as in its fundraising – that if congressmen were not feeling heat on the issue of HIV, they would find it hard to dedicate money to it. And (RED) certainly generated heat.

The objective

The original objective was to raise tens of millions of dollars specifically to fight HIV/AIDS in Africa. The entire 100 per cent of the funds generated by (RED) partners and events would go to Global Fund programmes that provide medical care and support services for people affected by HIV/AIDS. No overheads would be taken by either (RED) or The Global Fund.

The strategy

To get the world's most iconic companies to donate some of their profits on (RED) products and services directly to The Global Fund while also using existing marketing dollars and muscle to keep the issue of AIDS topical.

How the narrative unfolded ...

Phase 1 *The start of (RED)*

'Two pills: magical, astonishing pills, they cost 40 cents and if you have HIV, they will keep you alive' said Bono in 2005. 'I remember going to Lilongwe, Malawi where there were up to four people to a bed, waiting to be diagnosed ... but the diagnosis was basically a death sentence because there was no treatment available; drugs that you could get in any pharmacy in Europe or America. It was an assault on the whole idea of equality, that where you live can decide whether you live or whether you die.'

Bono was working with AIDS activists from Africa, and was hell-bent on using his celebrity as currency to get people in Europe and America to take action. When it came to the private sector, he and Shriver decided to take a different approach to raising funds, focusing on corporations and brands.

'I hate begging for money,' Shriver said at the time. 'In most cases when you go and ask for a corporate donation, they'll cut you a cheque and that's it. We wanted something that was more sustainable.'

Shriver's friend, the US marketing guru Mark Dowley, got his client John Hayes, the chief marketing officer of American Express, interested in the idea of (RED). They wanted to test the brand in the UK by launching a (RED) card, which would realize a donation from Amex of 1 per cent on the customer's 'spend'.

Within a few months the (RED) team, which now included the branding and design consultancy Wolff Olins, had created a clean-looking logo with trademark parentheses: (RED)™. A subsequent roadshow encouraged the first partners – Gap, Armani and Converse along with American Express – to sign up.

The (RED) team then set their sights on Matthew Freud. 'His company not only specialized in corporate PR but Matthew's connections and history with Comic Relief and Make Poverty History put him and Freuds in a unique position to understand the complexities around launching a pro-social brand like (RED) in the UK market,' says Bono.

Freud recalls his first encounter with Bono, which, somewhat typically for both characters, was on board U2's official plane on the way to a stadium gig in Rome at the end of July 2005: 'I didn't know Bono at the time but I was a fan of U2 and I moved in some of the same circles because I was friends with U2's manager Paul McGuinness and Bob Geldof. Somehow I managed to hitch a ride to their gig in Rome on U2's official plane. I was sitting with the roadies and the make-up girls at the back of the plane, when I got summoned to sit with Bono. He pitched (RED) to me, which had already been cooking for about some months and I said to him, "what you're suggesting isn't going to work."'

Bono invited Freud down to his house in the South of France the following week. 'There were the 15 people who had been working on (RED) mostly from the ad agencies and media planners,' recalls Freud. 'Bono said: "this is Matthew – he thinks it's a really bad idea, which is why he is going to be masterminding it".'

Phase 2 Launching (RED) – January to September 2006

Bono and Shriver were determined to stick to their plan of launching (RED) at the World Economic Forum in Davos in January 2006.

'We only had a few months to get ready for launch,' says Freud. 'In Bono's mind he originally thought there would be a very big ad spend from the partners. But I quickly saw that the money being pledged was much less than had been anticipated.'

Freud also saw that the partner brands were getting more from their (RED)-related product advertising and links with Bono than they were actually contributing to (RED) as a whole. 'I remember telling Bono that he was investing more of his own image than he was getting back from the brands. Bono and U2 had at that time never done any endorsement or deals with brands. He was personally investing £10 million of his own personal equity in each brand that was using his image in their PR. So I argued that it was only when we were getting £100 million in value from 10 partners that we could say we were actually "in profit".'

This was the point when Freud convinced Bono and Shriver that (RED) should become a PR-led 'movement' rather than be purely based around advertising campaigns; that good PR could amplify the inherently strong messages.

Freud masterminded the launch in snowy Davos on 26 January with Bono, Bobby, Richard Feachem (then executive director of The Global Fund) and the original corporate partners. At the start of the launch event Bono said: 'Here we are, fat cats in the snow,' only to correct himself: 'I should say winners in the snow. I feel a bit of a fraud, a bit of a loser because we are not winning in the war against AIDS. Every day, about 6,500 Africans are dying of HIV/AIDS and 9,000 more are infected.' Bono told the audience of leading business people and politicians that this was the reason why he was turning to 'corporate winners'; so that The Global Fund could make money 'in the slipstream, in the wake of these companies'.

In March, American Express launched a fee-free '(RED) card' where 1 per cent of spend would be donated to The Global Fund. And, when Gap launched its own (RED) line with 50 per cent of profits of this line going to The Global Fund, Freuds organized the launch party in London and a 22-page feature in the April issue of *Dazed & Confused* magazine.

By now Freud was an integral part of the (RED) team. 'It was a bit like running a political campaign,' explains Freud. 'It allowed us to scale up and down, from week to week, depending on activity. In the early years it was a pretty seamless team running the project.'

Shriver had set up headquarters in LA and, with creative chief Sheila Roche, started work on the brand's launch in the US to include a takeover of the Oprah show on October 2006. They, and the small (RED) team of six, were learning more and more about the mechanics of running these corporate partnerships. Equally, the team had worked out a way that celebrities could endorse the (RED) brand without endorsing specific products so they didn't 'burn their personal equity' by ruling themselves out of promoting any conflicting products from other companies. 'It was a cute solution,' says Freud.

Freud and Bono now agreed that the (RED) campaign needed a stronger 'voice'. In a masterstroke Freud arranged for Bono to guest-edit *The Independent* newspaper. The cover, designed by Damien Hirst, simply said 'NO NEWS TODAY*' and in very small letters at the bottom '*Just 6,500 Africans died today as a result of a preventable, treatable disease'. Based on this success, and Mark Dowley's introduction to *Vanity Fair* editor, Graydon Carter, the following year Bono guest-edited the June issue of *Vanity Fair*, branded 'The Africa Issue' and with 20 different covers, photographed by Annie Leibovitz. It featured celebrities dedicated to issues in Africa including Barack Obama, Muhammad Ali and Desmond Tutu. Several such guest-edited issues of newspapers and magazines around the world followed.

Subsequently a raft of new corporate partners signed up. Apple alone, which started with a (RED) version of its iPod Nano in 2006, now sells half a dozen (RED) products. Apple alone has contributed more than $100 million via (RED).

Phase 3 *2008 onwards*

'Post-launch it went a bit quiet,' admits Freud, 'but then there was Damien's art auction which successfully rebooted it.' At Bono's request, for Valentine's Day 2008, Damien Hirst had contacted the world's leading artists to ask them to contribute works for the auction inspired by the colour red and the concept of love. The auction, co-hosted by Hirst and Bono, featured major works by Banksy, Anish Kapoor and Jeff Koons. It raised $42.6 million for The Global Fund.

The partnerships and events have continued ever since. In November 2013 Apple designer Jony Ive and industrial design guru Marc Newson curated an auction at Sotheby's attended by Leonardo DiCaprio, Chris Martin, Tim Cook and Laurene Powell Jobs, which raised nearly $13 million for The Global Fund. Bill Gates matched it, to bring in $26 million from the night. Most importantly, that amount unlocked UK and US government matching grants which brought Jony and Marc's efforts over two years working on the collection to a total of $44 million.

In January 2014 Bank of America joined as a partner with a commitment of $10 million and bought a dedicated ad during the US Superbowl, which featured a record-breaking donation triggering mechanism – the U2 song 'Invisible' featured in the ad raised $3.1 million in 36 hours on the back of 3.1 million downloads.

Postscript ...

In June 2014 the Cannes Lions International Festival of Creativity honoured Bono with the LionHeart Award for his work with (RED) to raise money for the fight against AIDS.

The campaign goes on, and continues to tweak its operations to deploy its partners and assets most effectively. Some corporate partners produce (RED)-branded products all year round, while others focus their efforts on the two points in the year where (RED) pulls out the stops with events around the globe. These are World AIDS Day, 1 December, and a month-long campaign, which takes place in June.

But for how long will (RED) go on? Is there that element that almost defines a great campaign: a winnable objective? Freud reflects: 'I keep trying to convince Bono to build in obsolescence. For the past five years (RED) has only been channelling money to prevent mother-to-child HIV transference. We hope that by 2020 no child will be born with HIV. At that point, I hope it takes on a huge challenge or mutates into something else.'

ON REFLECTION

- (RED) differs from traditional forms of cause-related marketing in a number of important ways: it is based on co-branding rather than on enhancing the visibility of one brand alone; (RED) provides the 'umbrella' brand under which the other brands are embedded; the (RED) brand is built around the notion of continuity of support rather than just one-off impact; and the campaign links corporations with seemingly diverse business and corporate giving profiles.

- It is also that rare thing: a campaign that harnesses a diverse array of stakeholders towards a higher purpose: a marketing movement.

- There is a strong sense of vision and leadership, from such illustrious characters as Bono, Bobby Shriver and Bill Gates. There is also a sense that only a PR of Freud's calibre, experience and social standing could have pulled this project off via his strategic nous and his ability to network and form mutual alliances.

- (RED) has been criticized for not having an effect proportional to the advertising investment; for being much less efficient than direct charitable contribution; and for lacking transparency with regards to the amount of money going to charity as a percentage of every purchase. Some go as far as to argue that a retail middleman between donor and charity is unnecessary. Others argue that (RED)'s expansion into traditional fundraising techniques, such as art auctions (which in reality raised almost as much as the product partnerships), undermines its claim to be a different and more sustainable approach.

- Some even accuse the campaign of profiting by using these terrible diseases as a 'marketing' vehicle, for actually being 'cause branding' rather than representing true CSR. In the *Stanford Social Innovation Review*, Mark Rosenman wrote that it was an 'example of the corporate world aligning its operations with its central purpose of increasing shareholder profit, except this time it is being cloaked in the patina of philanthropy.'

- However, (RED) remains an innovative and constantly evolving initiative linking the CSR sentiment from all kinds of people, companies and pressure groups into a single branded movement.

- An enterprise of such impact and longevity based on minimal seed capital is also a useful case study in what a PR-led campaign can achieve. While product marketing from the (RED) partners has helped drive sales, the agency, Freuds, gives a powerful example of how an earned media strategy has the ability not only to amplify a good idea, but also to use editorial media to carry a substantial amount of the promotional work – and to create a bona fide marketing movement.

Chapter Eight
The audacity of hope
Obama for America – 2006–2008

Introduction

Barack Obama's first drive for the US presidency was not only a brilliant modern political campaign; it created a sea-change in the way all great campaigns – corporate, branding or entertainment – were subsequently run around the world. It is especially notable for its groundbreaking use of digital technology and for its clear strategy, rigorous discipline and authenticity of vision.

Why the campaign shook the world

Barack Hussein Obama genuinely only decided to run for US President 22 months before election day. He was 45 years old at the time, was born to a Kenyan and a Kansan, and had been a senator for just two years. And yet he pulled off a quite remarkable victory, fighting off both a fearsome and powerfully funded rival for the Democratic candidacy in Hillary Clinton, and then a strong Republican candidate for the presidency in Senator John McCain.

David Axelrod
Source The official White House photostream, photographer: Pete Souza

Barack Obama
Source The official White House photostream, photographer: Pete Souza

Obama's run at the presidency was motivated by idealism to an unusual degree and he won by mobilizing the young and ethnic minorities who had hitherto been disillusioned with politics. 'Organizing for America', set up by team Obama, became a 13 million-strong group of supporters who continued the campaign in everyday political and civic life.

The campaign's fundraising broke previous records for presidential primary and general campaigns, with most of the money raised online and in small amounts, and changed expectations for future presidential elections. Obama for America avoided using public campaign funds, raising all of its money privately from individual donors. By the general election the campaign committee had raised more than $650 million for itself, and coordinated with both the Democratic National Committee (DNC) and at least 18 state-level Democratic committees, to create a joint fundraising committee to raise and split tens of millions of dollars more.

Even more notably, Obama effectively broke up a three-decade sequence of presidents from the Bush and Clinton dynasties, and became the first African–American to take his seat in the Oval Office.

Why is the campaign great?

Obama for America was the world's first truly digital general election campaign. While the corporate and entertainment worlds were being transformed by digital technology during the 2000s, political campaigns had fallen way behind. Obama and his comms team, with the help of Google's Eric Schmidt and other advisers, changed all that. This was to be an internet-led campaign.

That said, the new technology and the social media mobilization were underpinned by 'old school' political techniques such as door-to-door campaigning, bussing supporters to a huge array of events – from local coffee mornings to huge set-piece rallies – and, moreover, brilliant oratory performances from Obama himself.

It was this effective blend of old and new that eventually transcended a campaign – evolving into an unstoppable grassroots 'movement'.

The cast

Barack Obama (born 1961) and **Michelle Obama** (born 1964), US President and First Lady from 2009 to 2016
Before running for US President, Barack Obama had worked as a civil rights attorney and taught constitutional law at the University of Chicago Law School from 1992 to 2004. He served three terms representing the 13th District in the Illinois Senate from 1997 to 2004. In 2004 Obama received national attention during his campaign to represent Illinois in the United States Senate with his victory in the Democratic Party primary in March, his keynote address at the Democratic National Convention in July, and his election to the Senate in November.

There was never any doubt about Barack Obama's leadership credentials. Obama for America was his campaign from day one.

His tight team of strategists were in awe of his vision and purpose. He showed extreme loyalty to his team, with most of them following him into government roles. In their accounts of the campaign, key advisers such as David Axelrod and David Plouffe attest to Obama's leadership, judgement, calmness and amazing ability to improve any speech or commercial in which he was involved.

David Plouffe (born 1967), campaign manager, Obama for America, then became senior adviser to the President

As Obama for America's campaign manager, Plouffe was the captain of this 'band of brothers', which pulled off victory against all odds. Since joining David Axelrod's political consultancy AKPD Message and Media in 2000, Plouffe had been Axelrod's younger lieutenant. However, from 2007 he was nominally the boss.

David Plouffe
Source Getty Images: NBC NewsWires/Contributor

Plouffe began his career in politics canvassing door-to-door in Delaware and Iowa and subsequently managed two US senate races. After helping elect Obama as president in 2008, Plouffe became an external senior adviser to him. In 2011 he was appointed senior adviser to the president (inside the White House) following the resignation of David Axelrod, who went on to start Obama's re-election campaign. In September 2014 Plouffe became the senior vice president of policy and strategy for the international ridesharing start-up, Uber.

Robert Gibbs (born 1971), communications director, Obama for America, and then White House press secretary for President Obama's first term

Prior to working with Obama, Gibbs had been a senior staffer in a number of Democratic organizations and campaigns, including John Kerry's 2004 presidential campaign. By 2006 Gibbs had become Obama's *de facto* political director as well as his communications director. And after AKPD Message and Media were brought in for the presidential campaign, Gibbs was still the 'man on the ground' with Obama. Known as a tough enforcer, Gibbs was also incisive, organized and fiercely loyal. Axelrod said that Obama had leaned on the Alabama-born press man heavily for his political and media judgement and when considering the team for the presidential drive. In June 2013 Gibbs became a founding partner of a new strategic communications practice called The Incite Agency, which he co-founded.

Joe Rospars (born 1981), chief digital strategist for Obama's 2008 and 2012 campaigns

After serving as a staffer on Howard Dean's 2004 presidential campaign, Joe Rospars co-founded the consultancy Blue State Digital the following year, offering 'technology solutions and online strategic services' for political campaigns. Three years later Rospars was hired by Plouffe and Axelrod to become chief new media executive at Obama for America. His colleague Thomas Gensemer, managing partner at Blue State Digital, was also pivotal. Rospars has been described as 'the conversation starter' in Obama's innovative drive to mobilize grassroots support and fundraising. Today Rospars is CEO of WPP-owned Blue State Digital.

★ THE CAMPAIGN STAR ★

David Axelrod

Born in 1955, David Axelrod was chief campaign adviser to Barack Obama from 2007, senior adviser to the president from 2008, then the senior strategist for Obama's successful re-election campaign in 2012. Axelrod was integral not just to Obama's two presidential victories in 2008 and 2012, but also to Obama's election as a senator in 2004. He has been described as 'a lobe of the Obama brain'. Having been a senior newspaper journalist, Axelrod understood storytelling and was a gifted writer, conjuring up the Obama slogans 'Change we can believe in' and 'Yes we can'.

Although 2008 was clearly Obama's campaign, the team would admit that Axelrod provided much of the DNA of the organization. Obama had known Axelrod since 1992 from the Democrat party operation in Chicago, where Obama's political career had flourished. In 2002, before he delivered a famous anti-war speech, Obama consulted Axelrod beforehand and asked him to read to him drafts of his book, *The Audacity of Hope*.

In an illuminating passage in his autobiography *Believer*, Axelrod writes about how he felt in 2008, in the heat of the Obama for America campaign: 'I had hooked up with Barack six years earlier at a time when my idealism was being challenged by the cynical, dispiriting exercise that politics had become. But my partnership with Barack was founded on a shared belief that we could do it a different and better way. Now I saw this big, hopeful, unifying campaign as a triumph of politics as it should be.'

Axelrod was brought up in Stuyvesant Town on the Lower East Side of Manhattan, New York. He went on to become a senior political journalist on the *Chicago Tribune* newspaper before becoming a Democrat campaigner and strategist.

Those who know him talk consistently about Axelrod's idealism and his genuine pride in his work. His media work is characterized by quality not quantity of output and his 'healthy scepticism' towards the Washington scene. Equally, he is renowned for being scruffy, disorganized and pessimistic but also for his strong sense of humour. In one legendary tale on the campaign trail his BlackBerry, to which he was usually glued, literally became glued-up with the glaze from a hastily eaten Krispy Kreme doughnut, prompting hilarity amongst his team. Axelrod admits to gaining 25 pounds during any campaign as a result of his snacking. In *Believer*, he writes: 'All this contributed to my sometimes cartoonish image as a rump-led, paunchy, food-stained savant. [My wife] hated that portrayal, regarding it as demeaning, but it was a source of endless fun for my colleagues, especially the fastidious and elegant candidate. Barack could spot a stain on my clothes from 20 paces and loved to rile me about it.'

He continues to be emotionally engaged in the Obama cause, particularly on healthcare reform. It was the passage of the Affordable Care Act in March 2010 that marked Axelrod's most moving moment of his tenure with Obama. He called the law's passage 'emotionally overwhelming,' recalling: 'I began to cry – not little sniffles, but big, heaving sobs.' Axelrod's daughter, Lauren, has epilepsy, making the legislation both personally and politically meaningful.

But of course Axelrod's achievements extend way beyond Barack Obama. He was formerly a top political adviser to President Bill Clinton and is now director of the Institute of Politics at the University of Chicago.

More recently Axelrod has become more international in his work, advising Italian politician Mario Monti during his campaign for power in the 2014 general elections.

THE CAMPAIGN

The context

The congressional elections in 2006 had been disastrous for the Republicans, signifying a shift in the US public's attitudes and prompting much talk of a 'time for change'. President George W Bush was by now unpopular thanks largely to the ongoing war in Iraq, demonstrating the United States' declining influence around the world. The national economy was sluggish and the Washington political machine appeared divided by infighting and scandal. It was the first time that the Democratic Party had controlled the House of Representatives for 12 years and only the second time it had controlled the Senate.

By 2007 the media and public were focusing on the next presidential election in November 2008. Most of the prospective Democratic contenders for president – such as Joe Biden and John Edwards – had already spent two years building support and the front-runner for the candidacy was Hillary Clinton, whose family had been building its political equity in America for two decades. The young, black Senator Obama from Illinois looked on with interest.

The objective

First, to make Barack Obama the Democratic candidate for the presidency and ultimately to elect him 44th president of the United States.

The strategy

Using 'Change we can believe in' – a classic challenger brand positioning built on messages of 'hope' and 'aspiration' – the strategy was to build unstoppable political momentum for such change through committed grassroots support and funding in small amounts (summed up by the memorable chant 'Yes we can').

How the narrative unfolded ...

Phase 1 *November 2006 to June 2008*

In the autumn of 2006, the week before that year's congressional elections, Barack Obama asked Davids Axelrod and Plouffe, business partners at political consulting firm AKPD Message and Media, if they would meet him in Chicago the day after the election 'to talk about the presidential race'.

Plouffe had first met Obama in 2003 before Barack ran for the US Senate. Significantly, Obama had told him that he was determined to win influence not with 30-second ads and clever sound-bites, but by building a grassroots campaign throughout Illinois. Obama now wanted to apply the same approach to run for the US presidency.

As well as Obama, Axelrod and Plouffe at this meeting to discuss whether the Chicago senator should join the presidential race, the cast included Obama's wife Michelle, his spokesman Robert Gibbs and senior Democratic campaign executive Steve Hildebrand. In his 2010 book *The Audacity to Win* Plouffe recalls how Obama set out a clear vision to becoming president:

> ... the country needed deep, fundamental change; Washington wasn't thinking long-term; and we had big challenges like energy and health care that had languished for decades; the special interests and lobbyists had too much power; and the American people needed to once again trust and engage their democracy; the country was too divided; and the middle class and especially their children ran the risk of having less opportunity than generations before.

Having weighed up the toll it would take on his family, on 2 January 2007 Obama finally decided to run for election. In his 2015 autobiography *Believer* Axelrod says he had warned Obama he 'may be too normal to run for president' but the senator had replied: 'Well, you're right, I don't need to be president. It turns out that Barack Obama is a pretty good gig in and of itself ... But I'll tell you this. I am pretty damned competitive, and if I get in, I'm not getting in to lose. I'm going to do what's necessary.'

From their experience in recent political campaigns Axelrod and Plouffe had recognized how the internet and digital technologies could mobilize grassroots support and communicate message, particularly at a time when the attention paid to traditional media sources was falling. When they looked at the task ahead, with a gruelling six-month programme of state 'primary' contests leading to the selection of the Democratic candidate, and with Hillary Clinton as the formidable front-runner, they decided on a strategy of building 'an unstoppable momentum'. Plouffe explained: 'We viewed the [primary] race not as a national campaign but as a sequence of states – beginning in Iowa in January 2008 and running through Montana and South Dakota on June 3 – with the belief that what happened in any one contest had the distinct ability to affect the next.' The plan was to throw everything they had at Iowa to disrupt Clinton early in the primaries.

The positioning would be Obama as the 'challenger brand'. The team realized that, although they might not be able to convert supporters of other Democrat candidates, Obama had the power and motivation to attract new supporters and new voters; to get young people and African–Americans interested, and to the ballot box.

Obama believed passionately in real political change and grassroots support. His team turned this into an innovative campaign strategy: they would mobilize a large number of volunteers to attract funding in small amounts; these volunteers would in turn mobilize their communities to vote; and this whole movement would deliver the Obama message on a peer-to-peer basis, engendering greater trust than by traditional media relations. Plouffe captures it eloquently in his book *The Audacity to Win*: 'We would build a ragtag militia to compete against [Clinton's] regular army.'

The AKPD experts recognized that many of these potential Obama supporters would be tech-savvy, so a priority was to build a website – www.BarackObama.com – that would have the tools for supporters to organize like-minded voters and to raise campaign funds. Social media would then be used to propagate the campaign, so the team set up their own social networking operation.

In the early days Hildebrand focused on the political side, while Axelrod and Plouffe concentrated on press, message and fundraising. The comms team was gradually being completed, with Axelrod bringing in experienced Democrat-paid media and polling expert Larry

Grisolano. At the same time Joe Rospars, who had run Howard Dean's online programme in the 2004 race, was made director of new media.

Obama's team was up against a Clinton campaign which numbered Patti Solis Doyle as campaign manager, the former Bill Clinton pollster Mark Penn as Axelrod's equivalent, and tough spin doctor Howard Wolfson as comms chief. Thanks to Penn's enduring influence on the Clintons, Hillary's campaign was built on 'microtargeting' – identifying specific demographics, such as 'soccer moms' and hitting them with relevant messages. Instead, team Obama focused on one big macrotrend: 'change'.

On 10 February 2007 the Obama for America campaign announced his candidacy at the Old State Capitol building in Springfield, Illinois. It was chosen because of Obama's strong links with the town and the state, because it was where President Lincoln had delivered his famous 'House Divided' speech, and because it represented the campaign's 'mid-western values versus Washington DC values' message. Axelrod, working closely with Obama himself, created a video to accompany the launch, distributed widely via YouTube, which consolidated all the core campaign messages.

Obama's speech for that icy day in Springfield was written by chief speechwriter Jon Favreau, but heavily modified by Obama himself – a brilliant writer according to his team. The 22-minute speech remains a masterpiece in relaxed-yet-powerful political oratory. Some 15,000 people turned out in the cold to witness a campaign which was already crackling with electricity.

By the end of March 2007 Obama's fresh approach to fundraising was starting to pay dividends. The team had tried a new type of event in Louisville, Kentucky, where alongside the usual glitzy fundraiser for wealthy individuals, thousands of 'regular folk' were invited to an Obama-attended event by local organizers, at ticket prices of $25. Three thousand showed up. The team decided to adopt this approach across the country. Many of the attendees became Obama for America volunteers, the vast majority being under 25 years of age. These events generated positive local press coverage and live footage was uploaded to **www.BarackObama.com** in order to show a groundswell of passionate young voters behind Obama.

This was the genesis of a new political phenomenon of 'citizen fundraisers' where grassroots supporters were encouraged to raise their own smaller contributions to campaign funds. Team Obama provided a tool on the campaign's social networking site **www.MyBarackObama.com** enabling fundraisers to keep track and to ask others to contribute.

The team had set a target of raising $12 million of campaign funds, but by 1 April 2007 the actual figure turned out to be $26 million, matching Clinton's fundraising at that point and sending shockwaves around America. The team admits this 'go against the grain' strategy wasn't an easy path to take. Obama had to turn down a lot of prestigious events and ignore easy-win sound-bites. He refused to pander to established narrow interests, preferring to speak on the big issues facing the country as a whole.

In May 2007 the team unveiled Obama's first major policy proposal on healthcare reform, which was to embody the candidate's and future president's fight against the political establishment. It also began using internet advertising to drive people to the Obama site. By June the campaign had raised another $32.5 million, this time outperforming Clinton. The Obama supporter database was already numbering 1 million, a quarter of them contributing funds, which amounted to a $10 million contribution. The two categories of people who made up the largest proportion of this were students and retirees, showing the breadth of Obama's appeal. The funds enabled the campaign to advertise earlier and more frequently than it had hoped, which was crucial because of Obama's comparatively low profile at this point.

In the summer of 2007 Axelrod and his team sent Obama a memo recommending a campaign slogan: 'Change we can believe in'. Obama and Plouffe weren't convinced at first, but Axelrod insisted it summed up Obama's authenticity in taking on the Washington establishment and media cynicism. It was launched in September and became one of the signatures of the campaign alongside 'Yes we can', which Axelrod had cooked up for Obama in 2002.

However, by that autumn Clinton's fundraising was finally reaching full-tilt and she was starting to eclipse Obama's narrative and nascent war chest. Obama's team knew they needed a major event and speech to shift the narrative back in their favour. The team focused on the Jefferson–Jackson Day dinner on 10 November, an annual Democratic event in Iowa. Obama said he realized he needed to 'give my best speech of the entire campaign'.

For the first time he memorized his speech word-for-word. To build atmosphere at the event, at which other candidates were also speaking, Obama's team organized a music event beforehand and uploaded internet footage of Barack and Michelle Obama and their young supporters dancing their way from the concert to the convention. Obama, who spoke last, delivered a barnstorming address: 'Our nation is at war. The planet is in peril. The dream that so many generations fought for feels as if it's slowly slipping away.' Axelrod sent a three-word e-mail to Plouffe afterwards, summing up the speech's impact: 'F***ing home run.'

The Obamas on the Oprah Winfrey show, 27 April 2011
Source Getty Images: Mandel Ngan/Staff

In early December, one month before the crucial Iowa primary, team Obama pulled in their big gun endorser. For a whole weekend Oprah Winfrey accompanied Barack and Michelle at local events, which drew a combined 60,000 people, and had the added benefit of appealing to African–American women in particular. By now Michelle Obama was viewed by the team as crucial to the campaign's success. 'Michelle Obama was another road warrior, lighting it up around the state', recalls Plouffe.

There were continually tough calls to make, minor crises and outbreaks of negative campaigning from both sides, but eventually Obama won Iowa by eight points from John Edwards, with Clinton narrowly coming third.

Clinton was to win New Hampshire, however, which made the remaining primaries 'a rollercoaster' for team Obama. Nevertheless, with the online fundraising continuing to pay off, the campaign stuck to its audacious strategy. In January 2008 alone it raised $28 million in online funding, and now had 650,000 total donors, enabling more advertising in the remaining primary states. By this point team Obama was actually able to outspend Clinton's campaign. In February 2008 Cornell Belcher, Obama's pollster, said: 'Obama's campaign is taking on the look and feel of a movement. This isn't just politics anymore.'

By March it emerged that Senator John McCain had wrapped up the Republican Party nomination and was beginning his general election campaign. All Obama wanted to do was get down to the real business. But the Clinton camp was still fighting bitterly and won the Pennsylvania primary by nine points. The US national media started asking why Obama couldn't close the deal. But on 3 June, the last day of primary voting in Montana, Obama finally sealed victory. Less than 150 years since slavery had ended, a black man had become the Democrats' nominee for president.

Phase 2 *June 2008 to November 2008*

After such a bitter battle for the primaries it took a while to bring Clinton and her camp onside, but once this was achieved Obama could turn his focus on his new rival, McCain. Team Obama's approach was to target those states in which he could credibly achieve a winning majority, modelling many different scenarios. Certain states would prove to be critical. For example, if Obama could wrest

Virginia from McCain, the state in which he lived, it would both limit his electoral options and send out a powerful message of 'change'.

'We ended the primary with over two million contributors and more than seven million people on our email list' recalls Plouffe. 'And though McCain had a core of passionate supporters, he had a very thin base of hypermotivated voters'. Plouffe set a target for Rospars and his team to double the 2 million contributors and more than 7-million-strong e-mail list in the remaining five months. Plouffe writes: 'We had to hope that the excitement of the general election ... and the intensity of the campaign's "big" moments – conventions, debates and unscripted incidents – would help spike the number of people coming to our site and signing on.'

There was an even bigger decision to make regarding funds. In June 2008 Obama became the first major candidate to turn down public financing of his campaign since the rules were introduced in 1976. The thinking was that accepting public financing came with its own restrictions and team Obama needed complete control and flexibility for its new approach to fundraising. With this Plouffe set the target to raise a huge campaign budget: $475 million.

The next big moment of the campaign was a brief but ambitious 'world trip' by Obama and his team, in July, that would include Iraq, Israel, Britain and Germany. For the last of these, the team organized a massive public event in Berlin, which was designed to position Obama as a new friend to Europe. To help with this Axelrod drafted in a specialist speechwriter and a student of history. Obama's Berlin speech attracted an enthusiastic crowd of over 200,000 people and was beamed to millions more around the world, demonstrating the hunger for a new style of American leadership. Axelrod says of the Berlin speech: 'The speech Barack gave had to strike a delicate balance, urging greater global cooperation without disparaging America or attacking Bush on foreign soil. If he appeared to case his country or his president in a negative light, it would backfire at home.'

Back home, Obama had to choose a runner for vice president and although personally tempted to go for Clinton, he finally opted for the less complicated choice of Senator Joe Biden of Delaware, who had a wealth of foreign policy experience and the blue-collar appeal to challenge the maverick McCain in this sense. In a masterstroke,

Joe Biden
Source The official White House photostream, photographer: David Lienemann

digital chief Rospars saw an opportunity to make this announcement exclusively by text to Obama supporters. The idea was to boost the number of mobile phone numbers on the Obama database and in the event 2 million signed up to receive the VP announcement by text. It was the genesis of the internal 'Be the first to know' drive, which was used to further motivate Obama's grassroots army in the months running up to the presidential election.

At this point McCain pulled an unexpected rabbit out of his hat with the appointment of relatively unknown Sarah Palin as his own VP. Palin was a right-winger from Alaska and team Obama hit back by positioning McCain as 'impulsive and erratic'. Nevertheless, at least temporarily, it shifted the campaign momentum to the Republicans.

By mid-September 2008, however, after the collapse of Lehman Brothers, the economy was becoming the major issue of the campaign. Almost counter-intuitively, team Obama ramped up its grassroots fundraising efforts. It communicated directly to supporters with 'State of the Race' videos explaining how the campaign was running and areas where more money needed to be raised. At the same time this money was being used on heavy advertising, both in target states and to target demographics, and to position Obama as a global spokesman on the world economy.

The final 'big moment' of the campaign was the upcoming series of presidential TV debates, from 26 September to 16 October. Axelrod was an acknowledged expert on presidential debates and drew parallels with Reagan versus Carter in 1980, which helped the former unseat the latter incumbent by showing a mature approach, which built reassurance in 'the new guy'.

Against the background of the global financial crisis Obama talked daily with former treasury secretaries Larry Summers and Bob Rubin. He also offered advice and help to the serving treasury secretary Henry Paulson, Federal Reserve chairman Ben Bernanke and congressional leaders. This not only gave Obama great ammunition for the debates, but raised his political credibility with the existing (Republican) administration, and ultimately the nation. Obama strategically had pictures made with financial experts Warren Buffett and Paul Volcker so the public would perceive him as having inside knowledge of Wall Street.

Obama's mature and thorough approach paid off and he stormed the debates, taking McCain's attempts to appeal directly to the man on the street – he mentioned 'Joe the plumber' 25 times during one debate – easily in his stride.

During the final month of the campaign team Obama's 'grassroots' drive reached fever pitch with the e-mail list growing to 13 million. It used a barrage of radio and internet ads, e-mails, text messaging, door knocks and phone calls to mobilize people to vote, particularly the under-25s. Plouffe recalls: 'Through emailed talking points, postings on the website and conversations with local field organisers, our volunteers were stressing the same arguments Obama, Biden, Axelrod and Gibbs were delivering on any given day. You couldn't put a price on it – regular people bringing Obama's message to their neighbours, serving as our ambassadors block by block through the battleground states.'

And finally, at 11 pm EST on 4 November 2008, Barack Obama was declared the 44th president of the United States. When the full count was complete Obama had won the presidency with 365 electoral votes to the 173 received by McCain. Obama won 52.9 per cent of the popular vote to McCain's 45.7 per cent. Even more incredibly, younger voters had turned up in their droves. Among people voting for the first time in a presidential election – or for the first time in a long time – Obama had won by 71 per cent to 27 per cent.

Postscript ...

Obama's 2012 re-election campaign and his two terms as US President warrant entire chapters on their own. But a glib summary would be that Obama's 'hope and change' agenda ran aground on the partisan Washington political scene. Obama wanted to forge bipartisan solutions that would remake American politics but encountered massive resistance from the Republican Party.

From 2009 to 2011, Obama could claim to have stabilized the US economy, passed his healthcare reform, ended America's longest running wars and overseen the death of Osama Bin Laden. But, as even Axelrod admits, after the Republicans won the mid-term elections in 2011 and took over the House 'everything ground to a halt'.

With the help of Axelrod's team Obama won another term as president in 2012, focusing on the economy and American's middle class. However, a defeat once again in the 2014 mid-terms, a newly aggressive Russia under Vladimir Putin, and new wars in the Middle East had effectively stymied Obama's change agenda once again.

ON REFLECTION

- First, there was a tight, loyal team with a clear chain of command, from Obama himself to Axelrod, Plouffe and Rospars. In a 2013 interview with British political thinktank IPPR, Axelrod said: 'I assembled a group that I thought would be both strong and coherent, and also just people I liked.'

- Second, there was a clear and fixed strategy – understood by everyone from Obama himself, right down to a junior campaign executive. The value of this, as in any organization, is that day-to-day decision-making becomes relatively uneventful. The staff feel empowered and the organization becomes single-minded, creative and effective.

- Third, Obama had the most powerful message of any candidate during the 2008 election. His message of 'change' was authentic to voters and struck a nerve with the public mood. It was this that underpinned a sense of 'movement'.

- Fourth, team Obama created a grassroots movement that believed in its own ability to effect change. In this sense it developed a strategic relationship with volunteers and fundraisers. At the start of series 3 of the US TV political drama *House of Cards*, Kevin Spacey's fictional US President Frank Underwood says: 'I've always said that power is more important than money. But when it comes to elections, money gives power ... well, a run for its money.' For this reason the grassroots fundraising ethos was critical.

- But perhaps the single reason for which Obama for America 2008 will go down in history was the groundbreaking harnessing of new technologies and media to both communicate and mobilize support. Mark Penn's work for Bill Clinton in the 90s had highlighted the power of data and demographic profiling, but Axelrod, Plouffe and Rospars took this to a whole new level. They used mobile phone text messaging and internet campaigning to build up their support, with millions registering on the website, giving their ZIP codes, being invited to events and being texted. And the genius was that these same people subsequently went out to voters in their community and articulated the Obama message. Team Obama had turned one man's vision into a campaign, but then transformed it into 'a movement' of tens of millions of people. It was a learning for many global businesses and NGOs, as well as politics, although it has yet to be emulated.

- Despite Obama being thwarted in his attempts to change the system itself, all those involved in this campaign strongly believe it was worthwhile, not least to show that it could be done. And thankfully as a result, he is unlikely to be the last politician to try.

Acknowledgements

Believer: My forty years in politics (2015) David Axelrod, published by Penguin Books

The Audacity to Win: The inside story and lessons of Barack Obama's historic victory (2009) David Plouffe, published by Viking Penguin

Chapter Nine
Campaign for Real Beauty
Dove – 2003–2013

Introduction

Out of literally thousands of modern corporate campaigns, with billions of dollars spent on them in total, Dove's Campaign for Real Beauty stands out from the crowd as uniquely era-defining. It is a campaign that redefined purpose-driven product and corporate marketing pre-Facebook and -Twitter, and then developed further in an age when content is shared via digital media and companies are quite rightly expected to be even more transparent and ethical. As such it has spawned many imitations.

Why the campaign shook the world

On a purely commercial basis, the Campaign for Real Beauty (CRB) played a role in lifting Unilever's annual sales of Dove-branded products from a level believed to be $2.5 billion in 2003 to around $4.8 billion in 2015 (Unilever doesn't release individual brand sales figures). At a time when Unilever was developing Dove as a 'masterbrand', with dozens of spin-off products, CRB helped it achieve 'relevance' and an emotional attachment among its target audience.

Silvia Lagnado
Source Silvia Lagnado

On a corporate level, Dove showed how a 50-year-old soap-like product could create multi-textured brand relevance on a global scale. It was an example of how creative corporate and brand marketing can – possibly should – become more authentic and impactful with consumers, who have become so much more demanding of corporations.

Moreover, CRB shook the world because what began as an innovative marketing campaign started and maintained a new conversation about 'beauty' around the world. It tapped into what women were thinking and feeling about the concept of beauty; about their self-esteem in today's society; and about how the media and commercial world applies pressure on women and girls to conform to social norms. Arguably the 2015 backlashes over advertising featuring female perfection (eg the 'Beach Body Ready' ads in the UK) may well be the direct result of the more positive message carved out by the Dove campaign.

The campaign's success helped change the way commercial organizations communicate with consumers. It added new energy to values-driven communications, which the likes of Procter & Gamble, Nike, Coca-Cola, Honey Maid and Chipotle similarly embrace. It also widened the definition of beauty, influencing many rivals in the process.

Why is the campaign great?

We should not forget that this campaign was creatively outstanding. It is notable for its consistent use of 'real women' in all its commercial communications. But there were some powerful and beautiful executions along the way from high-impact early 'Curves' posters of 2003, to the moving 'Little Girls' TV commercial in 2005/6, right through to the emotional film 'Sketches' in 2013. Inherently the media planning and buying was also outstanding, from outdoor stunts to short films that dominated the internet. It is a creative and media campaign that has truly resonated with both public and peers (few campaigns have ever won so many awards globally).

Also, despite beginning as a brave – and admirably integrated – advertising and PR campaign more than a decade ago, Dove CRB evolved to become an exemplar of modern, digital, social communication. 'Evolution' in 2006 was a viral sensation, before most people had even heard of the term 'viral marketing'. Team Dove (the Unilever team plus ad agency Ogilvy and PR firm Edelman) were experimenting with a combination of earned and shared media, often eschewing paid media altogether, right back in the mid-2000s. Fast forward a decade and this is still seen as an optimum communications approach in the digital age. Even in 2015 'Real Beauty Sketches' remains one of the most-viewed internet commercials of all time, with more than 170 million views. Admirably the campaign continues to evolve and innovate.

And in terms of 'thought leadership' and earned/social media campaigns, CRB remains the absolute gold standard.

The cast

At Unilever

Silvia Lagnado, global brand vice president (VP),
Dove, June 2001 to July 2006
Silvia Lagnado went to the UK in 2005, was promoted to senior vice president (SVP), and left Unilever in 2010 (see Campaign Star on p 180).

Alessandro Manfredi, global brand director, Dove
He worked closely with Lagnado, was later appointed global brand VP, Dove Deodorants, and is still at Unilever.

Klaus Arntz, European vice president, Dove
He was involved at the crucial launch stage, and later became global brand VP, Dove Hair.

Philippe Harrouseau, Marketing Director, Dove Skin and
Masterbrand Unilever, January 2004 to September 2006

Theresa McDonnell, Unilever director of integrated marketing
A former executive vice president (EVP), Edelman Consumer Marketing, she started in 2004 at Edelman and is now with Unilever.

Steve Miles, global SVP, Dove, 2008 to present
Miles took over from Silvia Lagnado as the campaign's driving force and took it to a new level in terms of commercial focus and digital innovation. It has been under Miles's leadership that CRB has surged ahead in digital terms with 'Real Beauty Sketches' becoming a global viral sensation and one of the most popular marketing case studies in history. The Cambridge UK-educated marketer, who has spent his entire career at Unilever, was named 'Grand Brand Genius of the Year' by US title *Ad Week*, alongside his colleague Fernando Machado.

Fernando Machado, global development director, Dove facial cleansers from 2010
Machado is the Brazilian marketer who reignited the campaign with 'Sketches'.

At Ogilvy

Creatives
Dennis Lewis (creative director in Europe during launch phase – created 'Curves' ad in 2003); **Nancy Vong** and **Janet Kestin** (creative duo, Ogilvy Toronto – created 'Evolution' film in 2006); **Maureen Shirreff** (group creative director, based in Chicago, from 1998 to present – created 'Pro-Age' campaign); **Anselmo Ramos** (creative chief Ogilvy Brazil – created 'Sketches' in 2011); **Steve Hayden** (global creative chief, based in New York, during launch phase); and **Tham Kai Meng** (worldwide creative chief, based in New York, 2009 to present).

Planners and suits
Daryl Fielding (managing partner on Dove, 1998–2008); **Mike Hemingway** (global account director on Dove, based in New York, 2000–2010); **Erica Hoholick** (global account manager on Dove 2011–2014); **Stephane Orhan** (managing partner, Dove 2010 to present); **Olivia Johnson** (planning partner, launch phase); and **John Stuart** (planning partner, 2005 to present).

At Edelman

Creatives and planners

Larry Koffler, EVP, Business and Social Purpose (began working on Dove in 2004 and helped launch CRB in the US – still working on the account); **Lisa Sepulveda,** president, Global Client Management (started in 2004 and still working on the account); and **Pia Garcia,** Unilever global strategist and global client relationship manager (started in 2012 and still working on the account).

★ THE CAMPAIGN STAR ★
Silvia Lagnado

It is only fitting that the star of this campaign, the marketing expert who was there right at the very beginning, is a woman. Silvia Lagnado was the mother of the Campaign for Real Beauty in every sense. It was she who, in 2001, came up with the thesis behind the campaign, who briefed the creative agencies and who drove it through the Unilever organization globally, sometimes against tough resistance. Her daughter Flavia, nine at the time, also appeared in an internal film on young girls' self-esteem that helped convince senior Unilever leaders to persevere with the campaign in the early days.

Born in Brazil in 1963, Lagnado joined Unilever straight out of university in São Paolo, where she had studied engineering. 'I had no idea what marketing was at the time,' she admits, 'but Unilever gave me excellent years of training in it.' In 1989 she moved to the UK to work for the personal-care arm of Unilever, called Elida Gibbs at the time, and in 1994 took on her first regional marketing role from the UK specializing in the deodorant category. Here she worked on the Sure/Rexona twin brands and the launch of the Dove deodorant range globally. After a two-year stint in Argentina, Lagnado moved to the US as the global VP of the new Dove masterbrand.

'I moved back to the UK, still on Dove in summer 2005. By that time the global brand leader had finally been given more power and budget internally. But before that I had to make the Campaign for Real Beauty happen mainly through internal influencing. Team Dove in the US was really just myself and Alessandro Manfredi. It was real training for me in how to use influence rather than money to get things done.'

The softly spoken and self-deprecating Lagnado showed enormous strength of character as one of Unilever's few newly-created global brand VPs in what was still then a male-dominated organization. When she took over Dove globally there was little consensus on the brand's direction of communications. But she admits that while it was daunting and exhausting, the opportunity for the brand was exciting, even intoxicating.

Lagnado was actually a pioneer for a new generation of integrated marketers, who could embrace PR and digital thinking alongside classic paid media. She says, 'I believe in ideas beyond media and I hope we will get to the point when everyone is digitally literate enough to stop the ridiculous separation of media. I have an allergy to siloed media planning. It often happens because there is no big idea, no purpose, no movement. If you have the right intent you can really make things happen. I don't agree when I hear people say "the future of marketing is content". The future of marketing is brands that are relevant, have purpose and are doing something exciting.'

In summer 2006 Lagnado moved to work on Unilever's foods business before leaving in 2010 to become chief marketing officer for the Bacardi company. The *Wall Street Journal* voted her one of their '50 Women to Watch' in 2009. In 2013 Lagnado decided to 'go plural', serving as a director and adviser on a number of company boards, including the Sapient agency, which in 2015 was sold to global marketing services group Publicis.

Lagnado lives in London once again but continues a truly global lifestyle. Her son is at university in England, but her daughter Flavia is at college in New York. Lagnado laughs: 'Flavia is now 21 and recently asked if she should have a nose job. I replied: "Oh my god, I've failed!"' Talking seriously, Lagnado concedes that the Campaign for Real Beauty may not have changed the world but believes it has made a positive impact.

Colleagues attest to her directness, honesty and passion. It was these qualities that enabled Lagnado to create a new sort of campaign – one that set new benchmarks to global brands to engage similarly authentically with their customers.

THE CAMPAIGN

The context

In the year 2000 packaged goods behemoth Unilever embarked on its Path to Growth strategy, with a mission to reduce its 1,600 brands across the world to just 400. A handful of these – mainly the ones grossing over $1 billion annually – would be given 'master-brand' status, meaning that they would become umbrella brands for an expanding range of products. Each masterbrand was given a global vice president with responsibility for creating its own global vision and then driving this across all geographies.

Dove had been launched in 1957 as an alternative to pure soap bars with the claim that it would not dry out your skin. Within a decade or two it had become an iconic brand, particularly in the US. In the late 1980s and early 1990s the Dove Bar was rolled out globally to dozens of countries and in the mid-1990s category expansions began (body wash, deodorants, body lotions, hair care). In February 2000 Unilever officially awarded Dove masterbrand status. At that time Dove's sales were believed to be about $2.5 billion.

Silvia Lagnado, who was moved to America in 2001 to become Dove's first global brand VP, was charged with finding a 'meaning' for the Dove masterbrand; a strategy that could be used to market its increasing portfolio of products. 'We were experiencing a lot of growth, but we were having a lot of issues with communication,' says Lagnado. 'We were still using a campaign called Conviction of Users relying on real customer testimonials – created by Ogilvy & Mather – which had been incredibly successful since the 1980s. But extending this campaign beyond the US was proving a lot of work. It had started to feel much like any other testimonial-driven paid media campaign, without saying anything very interesting.'

Dove had traditionally used 'real women' in advertising and saw its values as honesty and transparency, so this was driving Lagnado's brand thinking in 2001. 'I knew the brand well and loved its commitment to real women but I also knew this wasn't coming across well to consumers at the time.'

▶

Lagnado and her small team began investigating women's views towards 'real beauty' and how beauty was represented in popular culture. Their thesis, in a positioning paper called The Theory of Beauty, was that this limited portrayal of beauty was preventing women from recognizing and enjoying beauty in themselves and others. It was also becoming apparent that, in a world where female beauty was obviously highly valued, this situation could also impact significantly on women's wellbeing, happiness and self-esteem. At that time team Dove's research was turning up some disturbing findings on women and their attitudes. One internal study in 2002 found that over 50 per cent of women questioned said their own body 'disgusted' them.

The objective

As with any consumer goods firm, one of Unilever's aims was obviously to sell more Dove-branded products. But, as a firm with a notable characteristic for taking a long-term view, the Anglo-Dutch conglomerate was also trying to build a sustainable future for one of its most valuable brands. This meant giving Dove 'relevance' – an emotional connection – to consumers around the world.

The strategy

The strategy was to engage with Dove's potential audiences in an authentic way. So rather than the age-old product claim of helping women feel more beautiful, Dove's communications would instead be about more women feeling beautiful; in other words encouraging a notion of beauty that is not elitist but celebratory, inclusive and democratic. The strategy apparently came from the heart of its marketers who, beyond the obvious commercial imperatives, saw it as a moral and motivating mission.

How the narrative unfolded ...

Phase 1 *Launch of the Campaign for Real Beauty – 2003 to 2006*

Silvia Lagnado, the senior global brand director for Dove from 2001 to 2006, was determined to take an innovative and integrated approach to the marketing, with what almost amounted to a 'challenger brand' stance.

'We believed the brand could move from an aspirational view on beauty to an inspirational position for women about their own beauty,' explains Lagnado. 'The new positioning had quite a campaigning tone. We were looking at other iconic brands such as Nike and Apple that had had a cultural or social impact beyond what the product did, but related to the product. There was a sense of purpose – not so much that we could change the world but that we could make a difference.'

Not everyone internally at Unilever was supportive of the campaign at this point however. Some believed that Dove was ignoring its heritage and was in danger of losing the aspirational appeal that had traditionally been crucial to marketing any beauty product.

'Internal engagement was a challenge,' admits Lagnado. 'I had done a lot of work around the world selling CRB to the regions, but we needed to do something to convince senior people at Unilever.' So for an internal workshop, Lagnado and her agency team decided to make their own film on the self-esteem of young girls, interviewing the daughters of senior Unilever executives, including her own daughter Flavia. Lagnado got the cooperation of male executives' wives and daughters (without telling their husbands and dads).

Lagnado decided to brief advertising agency Ogilvy to come up with a campaign 'that would bring the CRB positioning to life'. She worked with Steve Hayden, the creative chief of Ogilvy at the time, to liaise with the agency's teams around the world. Ogilvy's creative efforts took 18 months to first see the full light of day. Many incarnations of the creative had clearly fallen flat with focus groups. 'It took a while to get the tone right' admits Lagnado. 'We didn't want it to be too worthy or too aggressive.'

Ogilvy in Düsseldorf eventually came up with the answer, producing some powerful poster work for Dove firming lotion showing an array of 'curvy' women standing in their underwear, challenging the notion that it is the classic size 10 (UK) model who needs firmer thighs. These 'Curves' ads appeared on billboards in London in 2003. 'The work didn't yet have the words Campaign for Real Beauty on it, but the heart of the campaign was there. We knew this was it. I hugged my colleague,' recalls Lagnado. 'I was eternally grateful to Klaus Arntz who led Dove in Europe at the time and was the one who briefed in and approved this work.'

Dove 'Curves' poster, 2003
Source Image courtesy of The Advertising Archives

'The ultimately iconic Curves campaign ignited things in Europe, but the US was to prove a slower burn,' explains John Stuart, a planner at Ogilvy who has worked on CRB since 2005.

The CRB campaign began in earnest in March 2004 – in North America, Europe and Latin America. In Toronto, Dove and Ogilvy organized a photography exhibition called 'Beyond Compare: Women Photographers on Real Beauty', which featured work from more than 60 female photographers including Annie Leibovitz and Peggy Sirota. The first advertising executions that used the tagline 'Campaign for Real Beauty' debuted at the same time, with a series of posters known as the 'Tick Box' ads, shot by edgy British fashion photographer Rankin. Ogilvy erected billboards showing 'ordinary women' photographed like supermodels.

Dove 'Tick-box' poster, 2004
Source Ogilvy

There was a giant billboard in Times Square in New York and at an intersection in Toronto (see above). They showed a curvy woman and a tagline asking 'fat or fit'? Drivers used their mobile phones to text in their votes to 1-800-342-DOVE, with the poll shown in real time on the poster site. The poll varied but was averaging out at 52 per cent for 'fat', 49 per cent for 'fit'. Lagnado says: 'We chose outdoor as the medium because the idea just cried out for some very public, very shocking media.'

To launch the advertising campaign, and to give it credibility, team Dove had simultaneously worked with Strategy One, the New York-based research and strategy arm of PR network Edelman, to create more robust research on the issue. This resulted in a survey of 3,200 women, aged 18–64, across 10 countries: the USA, Canada, Great Britain, Italy, France, Portugal, Netherlands, Brazil, Argentina and Japan. The survey investigated women's attitudes to beauty and well-being, and the relationship between them. The study was developed in collaboration with two psychologists: Dr Nancy Etcoff from Harvard University, and Dr Susie Orbach of the London School of Economics. Orbach was famous for advising Princess Diana and for her seminal book *Fat is a Feminist Issue* (1978).

In 2004 a White Paper on the study entitled *The Real Truth About Beauty: a Global Report* drew the following conclusion: 'Authentic beauty is a concept lodged in women's hearts and minds and seldom articulated in popular culture or affirmed in the mass media. As such, it remains unrealized and unclaimed. This idea of beauty appears to have been replaced by a narrower definition that is largely located in limited ideals of physical appearance.' Etcoff noted that: 'Only a minority of women see themselves as above average in appearance and only 2 per cent claim to be beautiful.' And Orbach wrote: 'Seventy-five per cent of women in the study would like to see considerably more diversity in the images of beauty. They want to see women of different shapes, they want to see women of varying sizes and they want a broader range of ages in the pictures of women than those who, at present saturate our visual field.' Building on the early involvement of Orbach and Etcoff, Edelman developed and ran an 'advocacy and influencer' programme (which continues to this day) targeting the 'two dozen' women in the media and entertainment world who they believed would share the campaign's philosophy, and sent them exclusive information packs in advance.

The powerful advertising campaign extended across the US and into the UK, featuring different women but always with tick-box options, such as 'outsized or outstanding?' or 'grey or gorgeous?' Dove deliberately made the often controversial results public to prompt media conversation. To keep that conversation going, the global Unilever communications and marketing team managed an extensive media relations campaign.

Lagnado says: 'I sat back and watched our executives do media around the world. It was incredible – as soon as even fairly ambivalent brand managers got interviewed by the press they immediately became committed to the campaign. I remember saying that the more they got interviewed in different countries, the better it would help each Unilever region embrace the Campaign for Real Beauty.'

Inevitably there was a backlash from some journalists. Richard Roeper, a columnist on the *Chicago Sun Times* wrote: 'Chunky women in their underwear have surrounded my house ... I find these ads a little unsettling.' But team Dove decided to tackle this reaction head on, actively promoting Roeper's piece to broadcast media in the hope it would create further debate. It worked. There were 60 items in national press and broadcast media, and coverage on over 200 local news programmes. Unilever estimated all this earned media exposure to be worth more than 30 times the bought media space.

Crucially, to give the campaign real authenticity Unilever set up the global Dove Self-Esteem Fund, which still runs today as part of the Dove Social Mission, with the aim of raising the self-esteem of girls and young women. The Fund produces educational resources for schools around the world. In the US the Fund supported Uniquely Me!, a partnership with the Girl Scouts to build self-confidence in girls aged 8–17 using educational resources and practical activities. The Campaign for Real Beauty website, which also hosted self-help tips and discussion forums, received 1.5 million visitors during this phase of the campaign.

This phase of the campaign reached its peak in 2005 with a highly integrated burst of activity. Unilever's media buying was designed to create maximum impact including on one occasion showing the firming cream ad with 'real women' in their underwear on every billboard in Manhattan's Grand Central Station.

Meanwhile the PR strategy was to tell the stories of the women featuring in the ads, starting with media in their hometowns. Edelman then built up a bigger story for *USA Today*, and subsequently used this to pitch national broadcast stories including achieving interviews with the 'models' on the *Today Show*. Edelman got a story on what was the PR holy grail at the time, Oprah Winfrey's eponymous show.

Lagnado and Ogilvy Toronto came up with the masterstroke of remaking the internal Unilever film about daughters' self-esteem as a TV ad called 'Little Girls'. This included a young girl who 'hates her freckles' and an Asian girl who 'wishes she were blonde'. And Unilever's US bosses took the decision, which Lagnado describes as a 'really bold move', to screen the 'Little Girls' ad during the 2006 Superbowl, which attracts the highest audience in US television, about 90 million people at that time, 45 per cent of which were female. The estimated media spend for this 30-second spot was \$2.5 million. 'Little Girls' became a global campaign with TV and poster executions in several countries.

The earned media drive also notched up a gear. Oprah Winfrey devoted a full episode of her show to self-esteem. Fellow TV chat show host Jay Leno ran a parody of the ad on his own show, cementing its penetration of the public consciousness.

Phase 2 *CRB becomes a digital communications campaign – 2006 to 2007*

The next phase of the Dove CRB campaign almost unwittingly took advantage of the advent of the new 'social' media way before most marketers and communications professionals had cottoned on. In 2006, Ogilvy Toronto was seeking to extend the campaign further by creating one or more viral videos to host on the Campaign for Real Beauty website. The first of these, 'Daughters', was an interview-style piece intended to show how mothers and daughters related to issues surrounding the modern perception of beauty and the beauty industry. With the budget left over from 'Daughters' Tim Piper, the Australian art director at Ogilvy Toronto, created another two-minute digital film called 'Evolution'. It showed the face of a normal young woman being transformed into a glamorous face on a bill-board by the application of make-up, hairstyling and, importantly, digital photoshop editing. The endline was: 'No wonder our perception of beauty is distorted.'

With an unusual strategy to eschew any paid media advertising, the film was posted on YouTube in October 2006, and within three months had been viewed 3 million times. With YouTube just launched, viral was still a relatively new concept in marketing at the time.

'There wasn't much science behind it. They just did it, and it flew,' recalls Lagnado. 'We hadn't originally briefed Ogilvy to use the internet

Dove 'Evolutions' campaign, 2006
Source Ogilvy

as the prime medium but we then realized it provided a very intimate conversation with our audience. Of course, unlike now, you couldn't buy social media then.'

But Larry Koffler, Edelman's SVP on Dove, points out that the earned media element was closely integrated into this thinking. He explains: 'We saw the media furore when Madrid Fashion Week organizers that year banned ultra-thin models from the runways. We pitched in advance to *Good Morning America* and leveraged the influencers we have built up over the course of Phase 1 of the campaign.'

Edelman's PR strategy was developed with Unilever at the key hubs of New York and London, but the agency provided 'PR toolkits' for Unilever offices and their local agencies around the world. The Evolution campaign was often translated into different languages and CRB was becoming more international by the month. Naturally, not all the commentary was positive and some media were increasingly sceptical. However 'Evolution' won two Grands Prix at the Cannes Festival 2007, in the Cyber and Film categories; the latter award was seen as controversial because the winning 'ad' had broken with convention and eschewed paid-for media.

By early 2007 Lagnado had moved to work on Unilever's food business. Team Dove, now briefly led by VP Fernando Acosta, followed 'Evolution' with another short film called 'Onslaught', also created by Ogilvy Toronto. It showed a young girl bombarded by media images seemingly designed to make her feel insecure about her looks. The endline was: 'Talk to your daughter before the beauty industry does.' While the film again prompted much media conversation and concern from parents, it drew fewer awards and more criticism, including a long-running social media meme that accused Unilever of hypocrisy for also making ads for Axe (known as Lynx in the UK) showing sex-crazed, model-esque women.

Phase 3 More product focus and Pro-Age campaign – 2007 to 2012

In October 2008 Steve Miles took over as Dove's global senior vice president and became the new driving force for CRB. There were some reports that the powerful advertising and the acres of editorial coverage were not directly leading to spikes in sales of Dove. Miles believed that the Dove products themselves needed to be more instrumental in the brand's mission. He also believed that the campaign needed less emphasis on cultural change and more on women's happiness; specifically addressing the idea of the 'inner critic' in women's heads. Once again Unilever commissioned global research to give ammunition and credibility to this campaign.

Insiders admit this period for CRB was somewhat restricted by the product lines themselves and the pressure to prove the products' 'superiority and efficacy' against competitors, which was a change in direction from the more provocative work in the launch years. This phase was exemplified by the Pro-Age campaign for a new range of 'anti-ageing' products. Again the communications focused on posters featuring 'real women' who were 50-plus, breaking the mould of anti-ageing products that are traditionally marketed to 30-something women. The posters had the tagline 'beauty has no age limit' – and featured barely-covered older female models photographed by Annie Leibowitz.

Maureen Shirreff, Ogilvy's creative director in the US at the time, takes up the story: 'I had actually just turned 50 myself, so it was a particularly emotional campaign for me personally. We were able to feature 50- and 60-something women who were largely invisible from advertising at the time. We wouldn't have been allowed to show such a campaign on TV, so we went with powerful posters.'

Oprah Winfrey was again so intrigued that she is said to have approached Unilever to effectively launch the controversial products via her show. There were also some negative stories. Controversy peaked when a professional photo retoucher told a New York reporter he believed the photos had been changed post-production. Unilever's PR team were kept busy, but the story was defused when a 63-year-old woman from the ads appeared on *Good Morning America* and said her image was natural.

'The models said they were proud to take their clothes off,' said Shirreff. 'And I was so proud of that campaign. It was incredibly well received and we won endless awards for effectiveness that year.'

Phase 4 *Real Beauty Sketches – 2012 to 2013*

By 2012 senior team Dove – which now comprised a core of Steve Miles, Fernando Machado who was global brand development VP (Dove Skin Cleansing and Care) and Stephane Orhan, Ogilvy's London-based managing partner on Dove – believed that while CRB had been highly effective in North America and Europe, there was potential to make the communication resonate in the rest of the world.

Steve Miles says: 'It was time to recommunicate Dove with a message that beauty should be a source of confidence and not anxiety for all women.' Once again the campaign was briefed out to Ogilvy teams around the world. Strong ideas came from creative teams in Paris, London and Shanghai, but the most powerful one came from Ogilvy São Paolo. Brazilian creative director Anselmo Ramos and his team came up with a tour-de-force piece of communication called 'Real Beauty Sketches'.

Ogilvy São Paolo created two versions of a film – one six-minute, one three-minute – in which a police sketch artist Gil Zamora contrasted how women describe themselves to the prettier versions described by others. It was an arty, emotional short film masterpiece that tackled women's self-perception with the endline: 'You're more beautiful than you think'. Zamora is filmed drawing a number of women, of various ages and ethnicities, sitting behind a curtain out of his view, relying exclusively on how they describe themselves to him. He then produces a second set of drawings, which are invariably more flattering, based on descriptions provided by strangers. The video goes on to capture the subjects' startled reactions upon seeing the resulting images.

'We hadn't planned to create a viral campaign' says Orhan. 'Indeed it was not a classic piece of viral content in that it wasn't humorous or provocative. Instead it was emotional. But when we launched it in a few countries and saw the reaction we realized its potential. After that there was a formidable mobilization online.'

In April 2013 'Sketches' was produced and uploaded in 25 languages to 46 Dove YouTube channels across most of the world. The video was launched using TrueView in-stream, TrueView in-search, YouTube homepage masthead, and search ads globally. Edelman masterminded the earned and social media element from Unilever's headquarters in London. As well as classic PR, the team encouraged audience participation via YouTube brand channels, Google+ Hangouts and a Google+ page.

The next month Unilever put out a statement claiming that 'Sketches' 'had struck an emotional chord with millions of women who recognize that they are their own worst beauty critic.' It told media that 'Sketches' had already racked up more than 114 million views, citing data from Unruly Media, making it the most-watched internet commercial of all time. It was also the most-shared video in more than a year, and the third most-shared of all time. At Cannes 2013 the campaign won a Titanium Grand Prix and 19 Lions in total.

Miles said: 'Sketches had taken CRB in a more affirmative direction, similar to the original Curves campaign, with a message re-dedicated to wellbeing and happiness. We found this made earned and shared media even more effective globally. There is a universal truth in this affirmative message for women.'

Dove 'Sketches' campaign, 2013
Source Ogilvy

Although Unilever doesn't release sales figures, by the end of 2013, annual sales of Dove were believed to have been around $4.8 billion globally, almost double the level of 2003, the year that the campaign started. And while CRB was only part of the marketing effort behind Dove, most Unilever executives saw it as a central pillar.

Postscript ...

One of the findings of the global study back in 2004, which was conducted by Edelman Berland (formerly Strategy One), that had launched the campaign was that only 23 per cent of women felt they were responsible for influencing their own definition of beauty, but a repeat survey in 2010 found nearly three times as many women now felt that way. It also revealed that self-confidence was increasingly a factor in 'looking beautiful'. Interestingly, the 2010 study, for which Dr Nancy Etcoff was again a co-author, found more than half of women now believed social media was playing a larger role than traditional media in defining beauty.

Unilever continues to evolve CRB. In 2013 team Dove produced 'Camera Shy', a film looking at the self-esteem of teenage girls around the world. In 2015 it produced 'Choose Beautiful' which appeared to film real women faced with the option of two doors through which to enter a shopping mall: one labelled 'Average' and one labelled 'Beautiful'.

ON REFLECTION

- Crucially, team Dove's vision – to redefine beauty democratically, so a broader range of women could aspire to the new definition – felt authentic. Lagnado talks about her drive for 'purposeful positioning for the brand, a positioning from the heart because I thought the brand had it.' In this sense team Dove had that rare thing in marketing communications, a genuinely 'big idea' in 'debunking the beauty myth'.

- CRB eventually felt more like a movement, and yet it came not from a charity or a political party, but from a maker of soaps and beauty products. Lagnado describes this as the 'democratization – where the brand is defined by the voice of the people rather than the voice of the marketing department'.

- Importantly, the campaign's 'authenticity' was backed by the credibility of a robust thought leadership strategy. This came from the early decision to establish the Dove Self-Esteem Fund, which exists today as the Dove Self-Esteem Project, running initiatives and providing resources to schools and other youth groups, and has educated 15 million young people and counting.

- An essentially 'media agnostic' idea was at its most effective when paid, earned, owned and shared media worked collectively. It could even be argued that in essence CRB was a PR-led campaign; it was issues-led, conversational in nature with credibility driven through the endorsement of credible third parties and experts.

- The campaign exemplifies how word-of-mouth marketing can thrive with the right mix of influencers and experts, as well as posters, online films, PR and social sharing. Even paid-for media were used to direct consumers to websites which hosted research, debates and discussion forums, hence further building the conversation and permeating popular culture.

- Above all, CRB will go down in history as one of the seminal digital campaigns. And very few internet-only films have pulled in the gongs, over many years, in Cannes and beyond, like CRB has.

- Beyond just the gender and beauty arguments, CRB was one of the first corporate campaigns to embrace social change at its heart. It was an attempt to move beyond cause-related marketing to put a single cause right at the centre of a brand's communications. And the messaging stayed largely consistent throughout. Other brands such as Nike subsequently changed their approach to women in advertising, instead featuring less glamorous, more 'real-looking' females. Unilever's arch-rival Procter & Gamble has also adopted similar themes in its marketing communications, producing viral films for the Pantene brand and a 2014 online campaign for Always called 'Like a Girl', which challenges clichés such as 'throw like a girl' or 'run like a girl' with aspirational images of sport and a healthy, confident lifestyle.

- It has not all been positive however. Throughout the campaign both traditional media and bloggers have accused Unilever of hypocrisy: how could it be fighting against damaging clichés on beauty while also selling beauty products such as skin whitener? Another jibe, which Unilever was prepared for, was that the same firm markets the Lynx/Axe brand of male deodorants, the advertising for which tends to show young men chasing slim, model-like women. It helped that Unilever kept the brands very separate, and used different creative agencies to promote Lynx/Axe (for which it used Bartle Bogle Hegarty).

- We should really let one of the women who worked on CRB, and fundamentally believed in it, to have the last word. Maureen Shirreff, still a creative director at Ogilvy Chicago, says: 'Unfortunately women are hard-wired to need positive endorsement. Our daughters will need the same encouragement, and so too the next generation. For this reason it has been an important campaign to work on.'

Acknowledgement

The Real Truth about Beauty: A global report (2004) Dr Nancy Etcoff, Dr Susie Orbach, Dr Jennifer Scott Heidi D'Agostino, commissioned by Dove, a Unilever beauty brand

Chapter Ten
Conclusions
A manifesto for
great campaigns

A lthough they span diverse sectors, the campaigns analysed in this book were selected and organized in a way that narrates the evolution of communications from the late 1970s to the present day.

Here are what I see as the essential elements of great campaigns, which have developed significantly over time. In each case I use one of my chosen campaigns to exemplify a particular element.

1. Clear vision, a unified team and authenticity

This is the starting point for any campaign and all of the case studies in this book rely on this firm base.

Margaret Thatcher's election campaign exemplified these qualities back in 1978/9. Thatcher has many critics of her personality, ideology and policies but few would dispute she was authentic; a politician driven by conviction. Thatcher had, in the early part of her premiership at least, a clear vision of the Britain she wished to govern. As such, she inspired vital loyalty from her campaign team.

With Thatcher's election drive, as with all the great campaigns that follow, this consistent vision and team provides for a robust and effective campaign. It is immediately apparent in the advertising and drives the PR campaign to win over key British media during a period of British history notable for ideology and partisanship. As Lord (Tim) Bell says in Chapter 1: 'Our unbending belief was that we would win the election by communicating a feeling – be it of despair at Labour, or hope for a better future – rather than a rational argument'. Such clarity of vision and authenticity is sadly rare among the thousands of campaigns we see around us, but it is shared by the campaigns in this book.

2. A PR-led strategy and consistent narrative (and the risks therein)

Tony Blair and the New Labour team had watched the birth of political 'event advertising' in Britain, conceived by Margaret Thatcher and Tim Bell. They had recognized how relatively little paid-for media space could create acres of earned media (PR) coverage if the creative work was sufficiently insightful and controversial.

New Labour adopted this approach but went further in prioritizing PR over advertising. This was partly born from political necessity in the face of such antithetic media. The subsequent communications campaign was highly strategic thanks to a group of ambitious and talented communicators in Blair, Peter Mandelson and Alastair Campbell. They ensured that every tactic, every story, every one of their executives was evaluated against a consistent narrative – New Labour, New Britain. And it is notable that narrative, or 'storytelling', has more recently become the buzzword in marketing communications.

Campbell's media operation was formidable to the point of being accused of bullying. He would argue however that they had little option when faced with such Conservative media bias. His disciplined approach changed PR forever, and not only in politics. Many in the business and political worlds admired and subsequently tried to emulate New Labour's rigorous professionalism in influencing the media, and the way it identified and repeated key messages.

Unfortunately, such as when Campbell was perceived to 'sex up' a dossier on Iraq and put pressure on critical journalists, this looked more like media manipulation or 'spin', which has been detrimental to the reputation of PR itself. It led to a consensus that the media were being warped by the activity of Machiavellian 'spin doctors'. Throughout the 20th century PR proved most effective as a discipline when it quietly influenced the narrative, but now some of its practitioners were becoming notorious in their own right. Unfortunately they had 'become the story', which must be avoided.

3. A collaborative rather than adversarial approach to the media

In its early days the campaign to revive the image of the British royal family was also guilty of spin. Again, when the stakes were so high and in such a robust political and media environment this is perhaps understandable. Mark Bolland, the first professional communicator to work on the campaign after the death of Diana, was faced with a tense situation and an aggressive media pack. As we saw in Chapter 3, Bolland's spinning of certain stories ultimately led to his departure. But from 2003 onwards Clarence House comms director Paddy Harverson began to adopt a more measured, collaborative approach which ultimately paid off.

By the late 2000s, and particularly after the phone-hacking scandal, both the royal comms team and the media were striving to find an acceptable balance between exposure and privacy for public figures. Clarence House worked hard to define the boundaries between public and professional personas, revealing each strategically and selectively.

We can see that this collaborative approach to PR and marketing becomes prevalent in other great modern campaigns. Its effectiveness is only magnified by the increasing influence of the internet on reputation; the growing power of shared stories, images and other digital content in robust communications strategies.

4. Forging partnerships and breaking down barriers

Mick Jagger, frontman and effectively manager of the Rolling Stones certainly had a collaborative approach. He successfully transformed the band's public perception through a combination of PR nous and a highly innovative approach to brand partnerships. In the early

1980s it was unheard of for a rock 'n' roll act to link up with massive sports stadiums, perfume and automotive companies.

Jagger and his team took collaboration to the point of challenging the traditional lines between entertainment and business. He chose partnerships with brands and people that helped make the Rolling Stones brand look youthful, vibrant and relevant. These coalitions were also highly lucrative.

The Rolling Stones case study showed that as well as requiring vision and leadership, a campaign's narrative could also derive from the coalitions made along the way. This was a concept further developed by many subsequent campaigns, which extend these partnerships to NGOs, politicians and pressure groups.

5. Embracing the evolving concept of 'celebrity'

From the 1990s onwards David and Victoria Beckham took the Rolling Stones' approach to marketing and communications to a new level, developing the concept of the global celebrity brand in its own right. It was to revolutionize both celebrity campaigns and those that partnered with them.

David Beckham's own ambition and vision enabled him to transcend football and develop a personal brand that was built around global sport, entertainment, corporate enterprise and charity. But he also relied on an impressive marketing and communications team, including his celebrity wife Victoria and Simon Fuller.

Fuller himself is a seminal figure in developing celebrities into bona fide global businesses. He sums up his approach to developing brand coalitions in Chapter 5. 'Our decision making was never just about the money but more importantly about the creative marketing and the global profile that they provided.'

Something that Fuller, Beckham and Jagger all grasped was the unique power of celebrity content when used strategically. Some celebrities have successfully evolved from specialist talent to franchises, and ultimately to media owners. Some, like footballer Cristiano Ronaldo have more than 35 million followers on Twitter. Others, like British chef Jamie Oliver, own production companies and run online

TV channels. In the future commercial brands are advised to treat them as equal partners.

6. Integrity and purpose

However, as the London 2012 Olympic Games demonstrate admirably, simply having access to great content and celebrity is not sufficient. From the beginning of this incredible campaign, Lord (Sebastian) Coe and his team realized that they were in for a long, tough ride to pull off a successful Olympic Games for London. And they would need an underlying integrity and purpose if they were to succeed.

LOCOG sensed instinctively that these qualities were crucial if they were to connect with a new generation of demanding consumers. They recognized success was being seen to deliver on their promises throughout the seven-year campaign: to deliver a great Games and to inspire a generation through the sport involved. With such high levels of scepticism, and a few crises along the way, London 2012 wisely opted to stick to its guns and rely on the authenticity of its vision and its key people.

As comms director Jackie Brock-Doyle says in Chapter 6: 'We wanted to be both brave and authentic. We would not claim to eradicate poverty, but we would give people, particularly young people, the opportunity to choose sport. So even when we took the inevitable flak along the way, they could never say we weren't delivering on what we promised.' Such focus and purpose enabled London 2012 to be lauded despite a long and gruelling campaign – something from which all ambitious campaigners should learn.

7. Building genuine 'movements'

Bono and the team behind Product (RED) also displayed integrity and purpose in their drive to raise awareness of global issues such as AIDS, malaria and general poverty in the third world. Team (RED)'s achievement was to successfully harness the sentiment behind forerunning 'movements for conscious consumerism' such as Live Aid, Comic Relief and Make Poverty History.

But with little seed capital, Bono and his comms adviser Matthew Freud were forced to rely on editorial media and coalitions with consumer brands and celebrities to provide the necessary momentum. Matthew Freud gives an excellent definition of a 'movement' as compared to a campaign: 'Campaigns are controlled, planned and executed and get a message out there. For a movement you have to rely on word-of-mouth marketing, sometimes prompted by conventional media, that people actively buy into. A movement requires a core piece of human truth or insight that sits at the heart of it; one that survives all the discussion and the endless retelling and sharing, and one that actually changes behaviour. Product (RED) set out to develop the movement of conscious consumerism that had been seen in Live Aid or Make Poverty History and get big brands to buy into it, with the message that we (the brand) care about the same things as you (the consumer).'

Indeed Product (RED) had achieved that rare thing – to get an army of consumers engaged behind an idea to the extent that they will change their purchasing behaviour and encourage others, including the businesses they buy from, to change their behaviour too. So what started as a classic campaign with clear vision and purpose transformed into something more: a movement of diverse people towards a single goal.

8. Optimizing digital technologies

When it comes to 'movements', there are few better examples than the one Barack Obama and his team created in 2008. Obama for America began as a campaign but his team and the media soon realized it had become something else. In February 2008 Cornell Belcher, Obama's pollster observed: 'Obama's campaign is taking on the look and feel of a movement. This isn't just politics anymore.'

But this was only possible because team Obama (including David Axelrod, David Plouffe and Joe Rospars) used a potent combination of classic PR, on-the-ground campaigning and groundbreaking digital comms. It was a narrative engrossing enough to mobilize more than

13 million Americans, mainly under the age of 25, and which raised $780 million, much of it through small donations.

The Obama for America drive reminded the world that there were now new tools at the campaigner's disposal. People could be reached at their desktop or by mobile phone. A political leader could talk to them directly without the filter of cynical media, and in an appropriate tone. More importantly, social media enabled people to share information with their peers whom they trusted more than a politician, company or even traditional editorial media. These social media could take on a life of their own; you could proliferate key messages or pieces of content virally, without the need to spend millions on paid-for media.

Charles Vallance, co-founder and chairman of integrated agency VCCP, says: 'Obama's fundraising campaign in 2008 showed how social media has facilitated the logistics of movement marketing and collective management. People could now sign up to and participate in a cause in a way that would have been inconceivable at the time of Live Aid. The principles of movement marketing probably go back as far as the Peasants' Revolt, but the tools have changed.'

To some, digital media are just additional channels. I have some sympathy with this view. Certainly one can apply many of the tried and tested elements of great campaigns to these new media. On the other hand, however, they change everything: information flow is faster and feedback is instant; the nature of content is more televisual; there are new types of opinion former such as vloggers; traditional patterns of influence and engagement become unpredictable; crises arise out of left field and at lightning pace – the list goes on. I would certainly argue that it would be difficult to change the world today with a campaign that didn't understand and test the boundaries of one-to-one communication and digital sharing. And the best campaigns are likely to employ cutting-edge thinking on these new paradigms.

9. Convergence and integration

All of the aforementioned elements of great campaigns appear somewhere in the book's ultimate case study – Dove's Campaign for Real Beauty.

Although it was for a commercial beauty product, indeed maybe *because* it was, CRB, for me, exemplifies a communications-led and truly integrated modern campaign. The long-running campaign was built around a genuinely 'big idea' – to feature 'real women' in all communications in order to 'debunk' the beauty myth. But unlike most campaigns it combines consistently outstanding creative work, high-impact media buying strategy, earned media for reach and credibility, and most significantly of all, brave new approaches to digital films and social media conversation on a global scale.

Underlying all these converged disciplines, however, is a sense of purpose and authenticity that is critical to CRB's success. Indeed, in such a digital, shareable, globalized communications environment, authenticity is even more important today than it was when Thatcher fought for election almost half a century ago.

This sounds trite, but you really can't fake authenticity. This is a particular challenge for most corporations who exist primarily to drive shareholder value. CRB's credibility derives partly from the fact that the manufacturer of Dove, Unilever, has long been a values-led organization. It also comes from the team behind Dove in the early days, with Silvia Lagnado at the helm, who believed the campaign was above all 'the right thing to do'. And it comes from team Dove's practical efforts to improve female self-esteem globally – helping schools with educational resources, linking up with women's groups and even lobbying governments.

Without this authenticity this would not have been a movement to address misconceptions of beauty, it would have been a campaign selling soap bars. That is the point.

10. Leadership, storytelling and creative flair

So what of the future of great campaigns beyond these fine examples? How will organizations be able to shake the world in 2020 and beyond?

The truth is that it is becoming increasingly challenging even to get to first base, which is to establish the required level of consumer and stakeholder trust in a globalized media world characterized by digital clutter, intense scrutiny and (often justified) consumer scepticism.

For more than a decade Edelman, the world's biggest PR network, has been using its Trust Barometer. The annual surveys have shown a gradually declining level of trust in traditional institutions globally, including government and business. Instead, consumers will show most trust for 'a person like myself', in other words friends or peers, which highlights the key role that social media will play in any successful campaign.

Richard Edelman, the firm's global CEO, argues that these 'tectonic shifts' in societal trust mean that organizations must campaign differently in the future. 'Business must move beyond the classic goal of license to operate toward a broader ambition of license to lead, in which it earns societal approval of innovations by listening and adapting,' he says. 'Brands are built not only through the tangible benefits they offer, but also in inspiring people through causes and content sharing. As activists and organizers of movements, such as the Dove Campaign for Real Beauty, the brands are forcing change.'

In a 2014 interview with the *Harvard Business Review*, Keith Weed, Unilever's chief marketing officer, said: 'In a joined-up, social, digital world, I don't think that you can separate communications from marketing. If you do, you're talking out of two sides of your mouth as a company.'

It means that successful organizations or politicians will have to evolve into what Edelman describes as 'living brands'. They will need to: display sufficient mission and purpose; invite participation from the community to become movements; be responsive in real time; be responsible for the supply chain, the wellbeing of customers; and help solve societal challenges. In other words organizations must stop simply talking the talk and start walking the walk. In a transparent world, communications can be used to listen and to lead – to actively change themselves for the better.

And still these brands will need campaigns that actually cut through the clutter of content and chatter and connect with consumers. For this they need creative excellence and visual flair. Otherwise they will not engage at all.

In conclusion then, great future campaigns will need to be: authentic, credible narratives, underpinned by big ideas and told with creative flair, and which hold up under the relentless, shareable scrutiny of today's connected world.

Other campaigns on the verge of greatness

There are reasons to be optimistic about the future of corporate communications. In researching this book I identified other fascinating corporate campaigns that are still relatively young but which already look groundbreaking and with the potential for greatness.

Since founding US 'fast-casual' Mexican restaurant chain **Chipotle** in 1993, Steve Ells has taken an innovative approach to marketing and communications, tending to favour word-of-mouth marketing over advertising, and viral films over 30-second ad spots. Since 2010, Chipotle's 'Food with Integrity' campaign has attacked factory-farming techniques and explained why better, sustainable ingredients make for more healthy food. Food with Integrity has featured beautiful animation films such as 'Back to the start' and 'Scarecrow' which were created by talent/ad agency CAA, shown on subscription TV services like Hulu, and integrated with a PR campaign by Edelman, which has prompted many a viral sensation. Chipotle continues to expand and is one of the best-performing shares on the US stock market. 'Scarecrow' won the PR Grand Prix at Cannes in 2014.

An example on the other side of the Atlantic is **John Lewis** – a long established British retailer whose ethical basis comes from a partnership model, with employees as mutual owners. In 2010, with the help of advertising agency Adam & Eve/DDB, John Lewis began producing advertising without any product messages but with plenty of emotion. It started with a moving film following a little girl's life through to becoming a grandmother called 'Always a woman' and then a series of award-winning pre-Christmas campaigns along the theme of 'Thoughtful giving'. Interestingly the short films were released online well in advance of appearing on TV, and accompanied by heavy earned media work, generating millions of views on YouTube. The storytelling is powerful, few products are featured and

John Lewis' sales continued to grow by a double-digit percentage each year. The 2014 incarnation, 'Penguin', received much creative acclaim.

From Danish origins in 1916, the toy brick company **Lego** has since the mid-2000s repositioned itself as a global entertainment brand, with an extensive and integrated campaign to champion 'creativity'. This campaign has seen Lego expand creativity workshops across the world, make a massively successful animated movie, and embrace audacious social media content such as the stunt at the 2015 Oscars ceremony, when Lego presented stars with Academy Awards made from its bricks and posted the reactions online. Hence a firm that made its first financial loss in 1998 is now a thriving and revitalized global business with creativity as a mission.

And they are not only found in the private sector. As Andy Polansky, the global CEO for PR network Weber Shandwick, points out: 'Public education campaigns have played a vital role in explaining important government programmes to citizens around the world and can often be the most effective way to reach and engage specific, sometimes hard-to-reach audiences.' The UK has run many great campaigns of this type such as anti-drink driving and the Talk to Frank drugs helpline. There are also public–private partnership examples such as the joint-industry funded Change for Life. On the other side of the Atlantic, the Got Milk? campaign by the US dairy industry has been exemplary over the past two decades, combining creative advertising with PR and stakeholder relations. Polansky explains: 'Earned media techniques and other public relations techniques have represented an effective way of engaging with mass audiences. They have also engaged with other targets, like the medical community and registered dietitians that in the end may have more influence in making the case about the importance of milk in your daily diet.'

The qualities of great communications professionals

Finally then, what do we learn about the people behind great campaigns and the blueprint for future campaign stars or communications professionals?

Perhaps the most inspiring aspect of writing this book was interviewing the nine 'campaign stars' who played pivotal roles in the campaigns that shook the world. I realized they share some important characteristics. While most could be defined as 'PRs' not all would wish to be – and some (Simon Fuller, Silvia Lagnado) are instead broader-based marketers. This is the case because, and as I have long argued, all great campaigns are integrated – and increasingly so. For the same reason only one-third of those profiled are former journalists, a career path that was once seen as natural, often essential, for professional communicators.

Understandably perhaps, for campaigns spanning the past four decades, most of these stars are now in their 50s, or older. This says something about a generation of 'baby boomer' comms professionals who have grown up with the modern media. Indeed they are typical of the executives who have built today's thriving PR and marketing sector.

Most are entrepreneurial and now run their own businesses. All are charismatic and thoughtful, often verging on the intellectual. I would posit that such characteristics are essential in professional comms today, where one needs to grasp and distil complex issues, as well as dealing with stakeholders from the worlds of politics, business, NGOs and media. Almost all these campaign stars are fascinated by politics and personally well connected. This is because the communications business has been forged from the cut and thrust of political campaigns, but also because PR is about influence and has tended to gravitate towards political power.

So if these are the current stars, what are the attributes required for future comms leaders? The evidence suggests that despite an increasingly ageist society where the cult of youth and digital experience is strong, sound judgement and experience will always be vital to successful campaigns. For sure, the next generation of leaders will have grown up with digital media and will be more technologically savvy, but this must be combined with the ability to relate personally to business people, politicians and specialist journalists.

The big change however, will come with the evolving comms channels and the types of content with which they will communicate. Look at the best campaigns today and rarely is it about TV ads or standard articles in the press. More likely it is a quickly shot clip on

YouTube or via a blogger or vlogger. It could be, as in Chipotle's case, well-directed films that are not shown on standard TV, but via the on-demand subscription networks such as Hulu or Netflix. It may well be via an app on a mobile device.

For this reason, outstanding creativity that works across many media will be essential to cut through the clutter of content and truly connect with audiences. Creativity used to be the preserve of particular individuals with ad agencies, but integration and convergence have changed that. Big, brilliant ideas can come from everywhere today: from PRs and digital specialists to media buyers. As Richard Edelman says: 'A great story will win if it is brought to life through powerful creative, with immersive live and virtual experiences and by leveraging the full force of earned, owned and paid media.'

So unlike the past, the great campaigners of the future may start as media planners, social media experts, even software developers or quantitative analysts. It is they who will be charged with conceiving the stories that will be talked about in a socialized, democratized world. It will be up to them to give people – voters, consumers or other stakeholders – a reason to engage with organizations or brands on an ongoing basis.

Ultimately tomorrow's comms professionals are multi-faceted, multi-talented individuals. They will help their fellow executives to lead organizations rather than simply managing perceptions – the old bedrock of basic PR. They must take a lead in listening to stakeholder feedback, predicting issues that will become major problems, making alliances with partners such as NGOs and fundamentally adjusting the business strategy to the changing needs of the marketplace.

But the single thing that will define the campaign stars of the future, from simply being adequate modern comms professionals, is a strong sense of personal purpose. If their work is to engage with – even change – the world, they will need their own determination to do good, to make things better. Shaking the world is one thing, improving it demands true ambition and purpose.

Index

Note: The index is filed in alphabetical, word-by-word order. Headings in *italics* denote a document or programme title; numbers within main headings are filed as spelt out; 'Mc' is filed as 'Mac'; 'Mr' is filed as it would be spelt in full and acronyms are filed as presented. Page locators in *italics* denote information contained within a Figure or a photograph; locators as roman numerals denote material contained within the Foreword.

CPSIA information can be obtained at www.ICGtesting.com
Printed in the USA
BVOW06s1215210716

456373BV00009B/24/P